SPECIAL SERMONS

ON SPECIAL ISSUES

SPECIAL SERMONS

ON SPECIAL ISSUES

by
George Sweeting

MOODY PRESS
CHICAGO

The use of selected references from various versions of the Bible in this publication does not necessarily imply publisher endorsement of the versions in their entirety.

Library of Congress Cataloging in Publication Data

Sweeting, George, 1924-
  Special sermons on special issues.

  1. Sermons, American.   I. Title.
BV4253.S835   261   80-26754
ISBN 0-8024-8207-4

To that select company of
pastors who attend the flock
of God

with appreciation to
Jerry Rice, producer of "Moody
Presents," Wayne Christianson,
senior editor emeritus, *Moody Monthly,*
and Phil Johnson who have assisted
me in research and production

Contents

1

The Energy Crisis

In Chicago one cold January, when most residents were fighting the snow, a young Christian couple went shopping for a dream. After weeks of looking around, they finally placed an order for a car—a new Oldsmobile. In March it was delivered.

It was their first new car, and you know something of how they felt—at first. But now the world in which they drive has changed. Their dream has been spoiled as they have suddenly found themselves short of gas, in an energy crisis.

Remember the last time you ran out of gas? Perhaps the gas gauge was stuck, or you just forgot to look. But there you were with four wheels that would not move and no help in sight. These days the whole world appears to be out of gas, and there is little help in sight. We are in an energy "crunch" they tell us is getting worse.

What is your answer to all this? Are you bracing for the worst, or hoping for the best? Does the whole situation say something to you as a Christian?

THE REALITY OF THE CRISIS

There are some people who believe that there is no energy crisis. They believe the shortage is not real—that it is a gimmick contrived to raise our energy prices or it is another scheme to "gouge" the public. Others hold that the crisis is real, but temporary. They think new sources will be found. They are confident that technology will discover new and better ways to provide sources of energy.

In his book *The Energy Balloon,* Steward Udall, United States secretary of the interior from 1961 to 1969, contends that both views are totally unfounded. He believes the American public has been misled about the potential energy reserves, as well as about energy alternatives.

Perhaps a more realistic view is that the day of abundant energy is gone forever, and unless we find hard-nosed solutions, catastrophe could overtake us. The issues are controversial; the problems are complex. There are conflicting viewpoints. In all the welter of figures, claims, and warnings, it is very hard to find the facts.

But the problem is important. It affects our future and our very existence.

What is the real nature of our problem? To begin with, our country is dependent on various forms of energy, expecially petroleum, and our demand for oil and petroleum products is rapidly increasing. With only 5 percent of the world's oil reserves, the United States owns half the automobiles in the world. We use over half of the world's gasoline supply and participate in half of the world's air travel. Our demand for oil has doubled every fourteen or fifteen years.

To compound the problem, the supply of available oil is limited and shrinking fast. Richard H. Bube, chairman of the Department of Materials Science and Engineering at Stanford University, believes that domestic production of petroleum peaked in 1971. He points out that 75 percent of all known petroleum reserves are in the Middle East, where they will continue to be constantly threatened by international politics, and he expects that we will begin to actually run out of petroleum in about twenty-five years and out of natural gas in twenty years.

There is also another factor. Even should we assume we can import the oil we need during the next few years, the price may soon become prohibitive. Oil that was selling at less than two dollars a barrel at the beginning of 1970, cost more than thirty dollars in 1980, and the end is not in sight.

That is the situation—an escalating demand for energy beyond our own resources, plus a shrinking, costly world supply.

Our attitude as a nation toward energy has been somewhat careless. We are incredibly wasteful of energy. In the 1970s our country, with only 5 percent of the proved world reserves, was consuming 30 percent of the world supply. And we are using more today.

We waste our energy in many ways. I was surprised to learn that an ordinary 100-watt incandescent light bulb uses only 5 percent of its energy in giving light. The rest of the energy used makes heat, which, of course, is simply wasted. And did you know that pilot lights on kitchen stoves consume up to one-third of the gas used annually by the average gas range?

We also waste incredible amounts of energy in the things we throw away. Figures from the 1970s show that the United States threw away nearly six pounds of trash per day for every man, woman, and child. The figure may now be as high as eight pounds per day per person. Virtually all that trash represents a tremendous energy waste. We need to be concerned that every 365 days we throw away 40 million tons of paper products. That trash represents 600 million trees—trees that had to be cut down, cut up, and worked with in a number of ways, all of which consumed energy. And that is typical.

In the next fifty-two weeks we will throw away 10 million tons of iron, over 15 million tons of glass, 8 million automobiles, 100 million tires, and billions of cans.

Even power plants burning coal or oil are incredibly inefficient. More than 60 percent of the potential energy used in fuel is wasted before it is converted to electric power. Nuclear power plants are even more inefficient. They lose as much as 70 percent of the energy they could pass on, in terms of wasted heat.

But possibly our greatest energy waste comes on the open highway. More than 80 percent of our working population drives to and from work, and more than half have only one person to a car. Many of our cars use engines that give us only 20 percent of the energy they consume. Not a few are getting as little as ten to fourteen miles to the gallon.

Compounding this problem of wastefulness is our practice of stimulating demand for more energy. Good business demands that if I have oil, I not only sell it for the most that I can get, but I also try to influence people to buy more. Or if I have a product that uses energy—cars, air conditioners, or appliances—I sell as many as I can. So demand for energy is increased. And the public tends to buy beyond its needs, anyway.

Our use of energy, then, links with our way of making a living. We cannot cut back on energy use without affecting our business and our livelihood.

Stewart Udall and the coauthors of *The Energy Balloon* believe that answers to our energy problem, at best, will be slow and costly. We must lay aside our wishful thinking, tighten our belts, and prepare for a time of major adjustment. They believe that we must halt our waste of energy, drive smaller cars, and drive them less. They believe we must develop public transportation.

In any case, it is clear that we must watch our energy use at every point. We must conserve, recycle, and develop every possible source of alternate energy production. In short, we must change our present life-style.

Time alone will tell how effective those measures will be. An energy-hungry society will do its best to find an easier way, but for now there seems to be no other choice than those crucial, urgent changes in our way of life.

THE ROOT OF THE CRISIS

A closer look at our energy situation suggests that the shortage has its roots in spiritual issues. The crisis is a reminder that our generation needs the grace and help of God. The measures we have so far suggested are at best temporary, stopgap measures. They do not deal with the root problem, which is corruption in the human heart. The ultimate solution to the problems that have brought about the energy shortage is a return to the God of the Scriptures. The only answer to man's greed, wastefulness, self-indulgence, and pride is the redemption that is available in

Jesus Christ. God's Word says, "If any man be in Christ, he is a new creature: old things are passed away; behold, all things are become new" (2 Corinthians 5:17).

Man-made solutions often generate new problems. The 1979 nuclear emergency at Three-Mile Island near Harrisburg, Pennsylvania, provides a good example. With little or no warning, a man-made solution to our energy needs confronts us with an urgent safety problem. Looking at the situation broadly, nuclear power would seem to be an answer to our need for energy. But instead we find ourselves confronted with a more imminent danger than the energy shortage.

God's solutions, on the other hand, create no new problems. Proverbs 10:22 says, "The blessing of the LORD, it maketh rich, and he addeth no sorrow with it." The salvation God offers in Christ is a real solution, not a cover-up or a cop-out. The person who comes to Christ finds genuine answers, for Christ says, "I am the way, the truth, and the life" (John 14:6). As the way, He is the answer to man's lost state. As the truth, He is the answer to man's confusion. And as the life, He is the answer to man's fear of eternity.

In Christ, God offers man the only real answers to the attitudes that have led him into the energy crisis. And the offer is to anyone who will trust Christ and receive Him by faith. "But as many as received Him, to them gave he power to become the sons of God, even to them that believe on his name" (John 1:12).

OUR RESPONSE TO THE CRISIS

How should the Christian respond to the energy crisis?

I firmly believe there should be a Christian perspective of the world situation. The Christian trusts in God in the good times and in the bad. The Christian will look to God to bring him through the stormy seas that lie ahead. Our confidence is in the Lord, come what may. He is sovereign. He can be trusted.

It would be very easy to put the blame for the problems of the world on the United States of America. That would also be inaccurate and very wrong. The problem is *the sinful nature of man,* not his nationality. Energy is wasted in Tokyo as well as in New York. Bigger is better in Sao Paulo as well as in Chicago. The "good life" is sought after in Paris, London, Southeast Asia, and throughout the Orient. Wherever there are people there are greed, selfishness, dishonesty, and deceit.

But how should we respond?

1. *Recognize we are stewards of God's creation.* Adam and Eve were told to subdue and have dominion over all the earth (Genesis 1:26-28). We must exercise greater care over the resources that have been given to us.

2. *Stop wasting what we have.* Many of us have been wasteful. If all of us would turn off the water, fix the leaky faucet, or take one less trip, the demand for energy would be that much less all along the line. We are living in a day when *wasting energy* is as much an act of violence against the poor as refusing to feed the hungry.

3. *Develop a simpler life-style.* Each day almost a billion people lie down to sleep inadequately fed. A thousand million people hungry! I am sure we agree that this is tragic, but some how we feel helpless to do anything about it. So we compartmentalize our thinking. We put it out of the way. In effect, we turn it off. And we continue to do what we have been doing. We buy things that are convenient to find and to fix. We eat more than we need—not all of us, but many of us. Expensive packages and containers become trash, and on it goes.

As victims of an easy life-style, we have unthinkingly perpetuated a problem that is fast becoming a crisis. We need a fresh vision of God and our needy world, which in turn will produce a life-style worthy of God's calling. Our model is Jesus Christ Himself, who, though rich, became poor that through His poverty we might become rich (2 Corinthians 8:9).

4. *Display compassion for the whole world.* The love of Jesus Christ working in and through us should compel concern for the whole world. When we learn that what we have is *all out of proportion* to what other prople have, it should make us ill at ease, uncomfortable, motivated to take action, to do something. We dare not live selfishly. We must retrain our self-desires. As the

children of light, we must reach out in Christian compassion to the whole world.

Writing on ecology, Dr. Francis Schaeffer points out that exploitation comes basically from greed and haste. In the end, he says, those who take too much too fast find the problems they have created return full circle to themselves. As Dr. Schaeffer reminds us, the church is really God's living, small-scale demonstration of the world as it should be. We dare not live selfishly. We must be examples of those who see and face the issue clearly, retraining our self-desires. We should walk as children of light.

Finally, the energy problem should remind us that we are in a twilight world. Human solutions have human limitations. We need God's wisdom, and we need God's grace. The clouds over our world today remind us that men are but tenants on this earth. Our existence here is not an end in itself. We are bound for an eternal dwelling place.

Let me ask you an important question. Are you prepared for what is coming? I do not mean just the immediate future with the problems of an energy crunch. Are you prepared for eternity?

In John 5:24, Jesus said three highly important things. First He said: "He that heareth my word, and believeth on him that sent me, hath everlasting life." Did you catch that? He said he that hears and believes has everlasting life. That means that you can have everlasting life now—you do not have to wait for death to find out that you have eternal life. Second, He said that he that hears and believes "shall not come into condemnation." Think of that—a promise that he who hears and believes will not be judged.

Finally, He said that the one who hears and believes passes here and now "from death unto life." It happens now, and you can make sure of it in your own life.

2

Abortion: Throwaway Life—Can We Afford It?

When is human life expendable? The question seems to have an easy answer—never! There is no life not worth saving. Two persons, or fifty, or even an entire nation will team up to find a child lost on a mountain, rescue a miner trapped by an explosion, or free a terrorist's hostage.

And yet millions of lives are being written off, snuffed out quietly and efficiently with scientific expertise. In fact, in the United States in 1979 the legal act of abortion caused more deaths than heart disease or cancer.

A talented Italian journalist, Oriana Fallaci, has become the spokeswoman for millions of unhappy women in her book *Letter to a Child Never Born*. In her book Miss Fallaci debates aborting her illegitimate child because the baby will interfere with her career. Finally she decides against abortion, but loses the baby by miscarriage after willfully disobeying her doctor in order to take an assignment. In short, she loses the child by choice.

Miss Fallaci acquits herself. But she clearly joins the millions of women who are experiencing uneasiness about their "right" to have abortions.

THE EFFECTS OF ABORTION

Abortion was legalized by the Supreme Court in 1973, and since then the problem of "throwaway life" has not lessened. In fact, it has multiplied astoundingly. Today it presses on the

American conscience as have few other issues. And it should. More than 8 million legal abortions are on record in the United States in the six years since the Supreme Court upheld abortion as a right.

It is not easy to picture the bodies of 8 million babies. Imagine if you can, a procession of abortion clinic attendants, marching in single file, each carrying what moments ago was a live fetus. They pass by you steadily, one every other second. Picture the grim procession moving endlessly, day and night, twenty-four hours a day. You would have to watch for nearly six full months before 8 million babies could be carried by.

A *Moody Monthly* editorial asks, "Have we been sitting, Lot-like, in the seats of the scornful, in the gates of our individual Sodoms, quite at home, quite unruffled, even critical of those who are so easily alarmed about—babies?

If the blood of Abel—one innocent adult—cried out to God from the ground, how much more eight million babies since 1973?"

Let me put it another way. In the years since the Supreme Court legalized abortion, we have snuffed out a population considerably larger than that of Philadelphia. Dr. C. Everett Koop estimates that Japan has destroyed 50 million preborn children since abortion was legalized there in 1948. And the epidemic has spread around the world.

Many who justify this form of extermination do so on the grounds of safeguarding human rights—the rights of mothers to avoid the consequences of conception. Others have a vested interest—the fathers who want no further responsibility, or possibly the doctors and medical assistants who make abortions a rewarding business. Taxpayers, many of them unknowingly, finance approximately one-third of a million abortions annually.

The effects of this harvest of willful death are far greater than we think. We could well be moving toward a society of middle-aged and older people. The present generation is not replacing itself with younger life. Consequently, fewer and fewer workers will be left to support a growing population dependent on Social Security.

Columnist Joan Beck recently wrote, "Doubts about abortion are growing, not diminishing. A kind of collective uneasiness seems to be increasing in this country, not so much among those who have always opposed abortion as among some who welcome it and still support it."[1]

But most important, abortion is affecting our relationship with Almighty God. Few nations in history have so invited divine judgment while needing God's favor. What should the Christian's view of abortion be? Should we accept what has been termed "the American way of death?"

THE EVILS OF ABORTION

Many argue that abortion does not involve taking a human life. They say there is no proof that life begins until a child is born. In its historic *Roe* v. *Wade* decision, the United States Supreme Court concluded that it could not decide when human life begins—that the fetus may be destroyed "for any reason or no reason."

Many believe, however, that in the decision the Supreme Court overlooked overwhelming evidence. One aspect of that evidence was dramatized and documented in 1979 in a historic feature on CBS television. For the first time in history, television viewers coast to coast saw motion pictures of the human fetus in the womb. The pictures made plain that even at the age of forty days, a fetus in the womb has a beating heart, a slender spine, and a brain that is already sending out nerve impulses. The feature stressed that this was human life, each one a "life never seen on earth and never to be repeated."

Recently, *Time* magazine made a similar point. "Even in the earliest stages of pregnancy," the magazine said, "the embryo is amazingly baby-like. By the ninth week the fetus is kicking and wiggling. . . . Its sex can be recognized, and at one point it seems to be trying to shield its eyes from the lights of the camera."

Is a fetus only flesh? Dr. C. Everett Koop, well-known for his outstanding work in surgical pediatrics, has this to say in his recent book *The Right to Live: The Right to Die:* "Once there is the union of sperm and egg, and the 23 chromosomes of each are brought together, that one cell with its 46 chromosomes has all of the DNA (deoxyribonucleic acid), the whole genetic code that will, if not interrupted, make a human being just like you with the potential for God-consciousness."[2] He asks a crucial question, "At what point can one consider this life to be worthless and the next minute consider the same life to be precious?"[3]

Later in his book Dr. Koop, who is a Christian, says, "As recently as 1967, at the first international conference on abortion, a purely secular group of people said, 'We can find no point in time between the union of sperm and egg and the birth of an infant at which point we can say this is not a human life.' "[4]

It is this human life that is the victim of abortion. Some fetuses are removed from the womb by suction, in a mass of blood and tissue. Some are destroyed by scraping from the womb, and some are drowned in an injection salt solution. Still others are removed by surgery not unlike a Caesarian operation, and the fetus is left to die if it is not already dead. In every case, regardless of the means, a precious life is blotted out.

Some people are quick to point out that the Bible does not specifically speak out against abortion. But the Bible does not specify every sin. It does say, "Thou shalt not kill." And the Bible clearly speaks of human life as beginning in the womb. The mother of Samson was told that her child would be a Nazarite from the womb (Judges 13:5), the implication clearly being that his status as a person began before his birth. Psalm 58:3 says that the wicked are estranged "from the womb." The implication is that even as unborn babies they are living persons. Speaking of John the Baptist, Luke 1:15 declares that this great man of God would be "filled with the Holy Ghost, even from his mother's womb." Only a living person can be filled with the Holy Spirit.

So the nature of the human fetus, medical science, and the Word of God all testify that the tiny creature in the womb is a unique and living person. If that is true, no one can commit abortion without destroying human life.

THE ERRORS OF ABORTION

That brings us to the real heart of the problem—wrong values that have been accepted by our society without regard to God's Word. What are some of those wrong values? First, there is *a wrong attitude toward human life.*

What is a human life? When God made man, He said, "Let us make man in our image, after our likeness" (Genesis 1:26). And the record goes on to say, "God created man in his own image, in the image of God created he him" (Genesis 1:27). Every human life, even in its fallen state, reflects to some degree the likeness of Almighty God. When man dares to take another human life, he lifts his hand in rebellion against the image of Almighty God. When Cain killed Abel, God said, "Thy brother's blood crieth unto me from the ground" (Genesis 4:10). The very universe records the violation of a human life.

God spelled out to Noah the seriousness with which He views the taking of human life. In Genesis 9:6, He says, "Whoso sheddeth man's blood, by man shall his blood be shed." And then He gives the reason for demanding such a penalty: "For in the image of God made he man." Never forget that God condemns the taking of human life and demands the ultimate penalty. Again and again the Bible tells us that judgment came to men because of blood guiltiness.

God judges nations, too. Israel—God's own people—was sent into captivity. Psalm 106:38 reminds us that this judgment came in part because the Hebrew people had dared to take the lives of their own children—a sin only a hair's breadth from the abortion we flaunt so openly today.

A second wrong value that gives rise to abortion is *a wrong emphasis on self.* Perhaps the most often heard argument for abortion is that the mother has the right to decide what happens to her own body. On the surface the argument seems reasonable. The mother is the one chiefly involved. Her future and well-being are at stake. But wait a minute. What about the child she has helped conceive? What about the obligation to the human life already conceived? What about the future and well-being of the unborn child? Are not his rights to be considered?

God gave the sex relationship to strengthen the marriage bond and to bless the home with children. No privilege is more sacred than that of bringing a new life into the world. No privilege should be exercised more carefully. And it should be viewed as a holy responsibility.

The Word of God says plainly that sex is for marriage only. Abortion would virtually disappear tomorrow if it were not for the willful violation of God's great charter of marriage and purity. The abortion problem begins with a rebellion that says, "I will do as I please for pleasure. I reject the limits prescribed by God in favor of personal satisfaction."

And that is the essence of the wrong values of which we are speaking. The root of all wrong value systems is a rebellious attitude toward God.

To put one's will above God's will, one's rights above God's rights, is to rebel against the sovereign of the universe. You cannot seize sovereignty for yourself without challenging Almighty God. That is what Satan did in his fall. Isaiah 14 describes how Satan went from being God's highest angel to become the enemy and deceiver we know him to be. In verse 13 God, speaking to Lucifer (Satan's name before he fell), says, "Thou hast said in thine heart, I will ascend into heaven, I will exalt my throne above the stars of God. . . . I will be like the Most High. Yet thou shalt be brought down to hell."

When we flout the will of God, we are walking in the footsteps of a doomed and defeated Satan. We are not the Creator; we are His creatures. We are not God, but people subject to His will and wishes.

For generations our nation has pushed aside the Bible. We have defied the voice of God. We challenge Him at our peril. Pride and rebellion are deadly sins. Part of their harvest today is the tragic and bloody snuffing out of millions of tiny lives.

Although we have made abortion legal, although we have made

it respectable, although we have made it commonplace, the fact—the sin—is unchanged. Like Cain, we are daring to strike down human life, life with potential, life made in the image of Almighty God.

"But," someone will say, "is abortion *always* wrong?" "Always" is a broad and sweeping word. There are difficult questions we have not been able to touch upon in this brief chapter. For example, what about defective babies? What about abortion in the wake of rape?

Those are special circumstances that represent only a small fraction of the total number of abortions, and there are answers for even such problems. We can trust God with the hard situations in our lives if we set ourselves to do His will where it is clear. We cannot expect His help or blessing if we ignore His Word and set aside His precepts.

And God's will seems clearly to stand in opposition to the wanton destruction of precious lives.

The heart of the abortion issue is stated by R. F. Gardner in a booklet published by the *Christian Medical Society Journal.* He writes, "From the moment of conception the couple concerned have not the option whether a proffered gift be accepted, but rather whether an already bestowed gift should be spurned." That is the issue—what will we do with a human life that has been given to our keeping?

Meanwhile abortion, like all sin, is not standing still. The tide is rising fast. Judicial decisions continue to make abortions easy, even for teenagers and wards of local government. England is looking forward to abortion kits for home use, within a year or two.

In this country many believe that only an antiabortion amendment will change the situation. If so, let's get behind it.

I am well aware that few who read these pages have had or will have responsibility for the abortion crisis. But we are guilty if we fail to raise our voices in opposition. God's judgment is not far from any nation that complacently accepts the slaughter of its unborn babies. Once His judgment falls, it will be too late.

May we stop being neutral on this issue. If abortion is wrong, we cannot keep silent. Besides taking a stand, we need to help others realize what is happening—and put our influence as Christians where it will count.

NOTES

1. Joan Beck, *Chicago Tribune,* 31 January 1977.
2. C. Everett Koop, *The Right to Live: The Right to Die* (Wheaton, Ill.: Tyndale, 1976).
3. Ibid.
4. Ibid.

3

Is the Church Unfair to Women?

Is the church behind the times in its attitudes toward women? A growing number answer, "Yes!" Too long, they say, we have restricted women. It is time, and past time, for a change. And change, they believe, is on the way.

What should the Bible-believing Christian say about equal rights for women within the church? How should church leaders respond, and what should be the attitude of Christian women?

THE WORLD AND WOMEN'S RIGHTS—A CONTROVERSIAL ISSUE

Since 1963 when Betty Friedan published her book *The Feminine Mystique,* the battle for women's rights has touched virtually every aspect of our national life. Now it is touching the church, and it brings up a difficult question—are women underprivileged in the Christian church?

Some believe with fervor that they are. In 1976 that conviction prompted the Episcopal church to vote in favor of ordaining women. A minority of the group reacted in dismay. Two years later, a hundred parishes broke away to form a new denomination.[1]

In 1974 the ordination of women was the most important religious news story of the year, according to a vote of the Religious Newswriters Association. The move toward women's ordination outranked such headlined stories as the moral issues of Watergate, the world hunger crisis, and the sensational aspects of exorcism.[2]

Today the tensions concerning the role of women in the church are even greater. Church leaders are asking if we have been unfair to women. Books on the subject are being written. As women remove the barriers to once-forbidden secular occupations, some church leaders are upset because they believe the church is lagging far behind. They believe women are discriminated against by being denied positions of equal leadership in the church. What is the situation? Although the number of ordained women is on the increase, the total number is small. About seventy American church bodies permit ordination of women, but many of those are small denominations.

Fewer than 1 percent of American Baptist, United Methodist, Presbyterian, and Disciples of Christ clergy are women. Southern Baptists, the largest Protestant denomination, having over 35,000 churches, have fewer than twenty ordained women in the ministry.[3] In a number of other groups committed to the Bible, ordination of women is opposed.

The critics argue that churches are steeped in prejudice and that it is high time they become enlightened. On the surface, the arguments may seem convincing. Barring women from the ministry, it is argued, presumes inferiority and is rank discrimination. Women are proving themselves in every other line of work. Why should they not serve as pastors? Many women equal or outstrip the men in gifts and abilities. The church, we are told, is missing out by not letting them use their talents.

Some hold that the requirements for pastors outlined in the Scriptures have been grossly misinterpreted—that they merely reflect cultural prejudices of the day, or perhaps of the apostle Paul. Society sees a whole new world for women today, they argue. So should the church.

How should the church respond to such pressure? What shall we say to sincere, dedicated young women who want to serve their Lord?

Are there satisfying answers? I am glad there are.

As we turn to the Bible to see what it says concerning women and the church, we find today's pressures have arisen from several basic misunderstandings. First, there is a basic error in understanding the scope and nature of the differences between the sexes. The Bible nowhere teaches that men are superior to women, but it does teach that they are different.

God created the woman at a different time and in a different way. In creating woman, He did not make a carbon copy of what He had already made. He fashioned a personality and spirit that would complement man and supply qualities man lacked.

The tendency today is to assume that except for physical differences, men and women come from the same, unchanging mold. Therefore they are to be competitive. But that is not God's intent. God created men and women to work together, not to compete. But He gave them different functions.

Man is at his best as an initiator—when he plans, leads, risks, and strives. Woman is made to reach her greatest potential when she rests on man's provision and supports him in his efforts.

We commit a basic error when we try to sweep this difference under the rug. It may appear to succeed for a time, but in the end we violate something elemental in our inner structure.

A second mistake in thinking there should be equal authority for men and women in the church rises from failure to see the difference between one's status and his role. As men and women are different, so God has made clear that they were made for different functions. In the church, as in the home, men and women are called to serve in different ways.

The New Testament makes clear that administration is a man's calling. Women are called to assist, helping as only they can in accomplishing the work. Some administrators of the early church bore the title *elder*. Others were designated *deacon*. Qualifications spelled out for both offices make it absolutely clear that both were always men.

In harmony with this principle, the apostle Paul in 1 Timothy 2:12 plainly writes, "But I suffer not a woman to teach, nor to usurp authority over the man, but to be in silence." (He gives two reasons. First, woman was not created to be independent; she was created after Adam to be his helper. Second, the woman had been the first to give place to sin.)

And so God has assigned leadership in the church, as well as in the family, to the man. His office is not a badge of honor; it is a mantle of responsibility. Men make a mistake to think their headship makes them superior. Women make as serious a mistake to assume their role makes them in any way inferior.

Jesus Christ clearly showed His regard for women during His earthly ministry. He sought out the woman of Samaria. He spent much time in the home of Mary and Martha. Luke 8 speaks of "certain women" whom He had healed and who, in turn, "ministered to him of their substance."

It was to women that He first appeared after His resurrection. Women were present in the upper room as the disciples waited for the Holy Spirit, and they, too, were filled when the Spirit came.

As if to make their standing clear, Galatians 3:28 seems to say that there are no distinctions in status in Christ. Paul writes, "There is neither Jew nor Greek, there is neither bond nor free, there is neither male nor female: for ye are all one in Christ Jesus."

Of course Jews still are Jews, Greeks still are Greeks, slaves still are subject to their masters. But all have equal status with Christ who loved them and gave Himself for them. The ground is level at the cross. Women matter as much as men, but we are called to different tasks.

A third reason for thinking that women should have more leadership in the church grows out of failure to understand the nature of Christ's church. The church is not a human organization to be conducted like a secular business enterprise. It is not a democratic organization to be run by majority rules. It is a spiritual body composed of those redeemed by Jesus Christ, persons made new creatures and brought into personal union with the Savior. It is a living organism, a spiritual family. In fact, the apostle Paul in various places speaks of the church as "the household of faith," "the household of God," and "the house of God" (Galatians 6:10; Ephesians 2:19; 1 Timothy 3:15).

As head of His family, Jesus Christ is entitled to set over it whom He will. And Scripture makes clear that in the local church, as in the individual home, it is His will that men should plan, care for, and protect the local congregation.

In a recent *His* magazine interview, Elisabeth Elliot makes an interesting point. Positions of leadership in the church are not, she says, rewards for competence. They are not earned or assigned purely on the basis of ability. They are assigned sovereignly by God. Those who take positions of authority in the church must be ordained by God. And God's Word makes abundantly clear that it is His will to have men in positions of leadership.[4]

Do not be misled by arguments that the Scriptures are influenced by cultural bias. Second Timothy 3:16 teaches that all Scripture is given by inspiration. In other words, it came forth from God like His very breath. God Himself speaks through the Bible, and the thoughts conveyed are exactly what God wants us to know and follow. God would not allow Paul—or any other writer—to dilute the truth of Scripture by adding personal opinion or cultural bias.

And by the same token, we must not be guilty of diluting the truth of Scripture ourselves by trying to limit its clear teaching to an isolated cultural situation. And we must resist attempts by the world to force on the church the secular thinking of our day.

CHRISTIAN WOMEN AND WOMEN'S RIGHTS— A CONSECRATED ATTITUDE

Many who argue that scriptural guidelines be set aside in favor of so-called equal rights fail to realize another fact—that Christian satisfaction comes not from title or position but from faithfulness in service.

From the church's early days, that kind of satisfaction has been experienced by women as well as men. Since apostolic times, women have found fulfillment in the church. In Romans 16, Paul writes of "Phebe our sister, which is a servant of the church which is at Cenchrea." Phebe found honor and fulfillment in effective service.

Paul also commends three women, Tryphena, Tryphosa, and Persis, who "did labor much in the Lord." In Philippians he speaks of Euodias and Syntyche as "fellow workers in the Lord." Priscilla, who ably reinforced her husband, Aquila, in instructing Apollos, is warmly commended by Paul. She knew how to minister—even to teach—in the authority framework of the Scripture.

Such ministry is possible for any women. But the usurpation of authority is forbidden women in the church. Women are not to attempt to rule either directly or by authoritative preaching or teaching. They are not to contend in church discussions.

But women can declare the gospel, teach where authority over men is not involved, witness, and carry the good news of salvation to the ends of the earth.

Sisters in Christ, do you want the blessing of God in ministry? Do you long to share in the work committed to the church? You can. But always remember the Bible pattern—God reserves authority for men. In all other places you can help as God allows. Do all you can within the framework of God's pattern. God will bless and make you fruitful beyond all that you could ask or think.

In some respects your gifts and insights may be superior to the men who are in leadership positions. Help and encourage them. Leaders are responsible to Christ for what they have to give. You are responsible for what God wants from you.

The well-being of God's work can be severely damaged when either men or women fail to recognize and fill the roles God has for them within His church.

The world has its ideas of who should lead the church. Those who do not understand will wave banners of new equality. They will minimize and rationalize. The world does not appreciate God's will or His purpose in the church.

But the Christian understands and knows God's way is best. We know that women are equal to men in God's sight and that

God merely reserves the right to assign roles in the church according to His wisdom and His will. We must resist the pressure to rebel against God's way.

NOTES

1. *Time,* 13 February 1978, p. 60.
2. Sarah Frances Anders, "The Role of Women in American Religion," *Southwestern Journal of Theology* (Spring 1976), p. 55.
3. Ibid.
4. Elisabeth Elliot, *His* (January 1978), p. 20.

4

Is Capital Punishment Biblical?

"The issue that won't go away." That is how a national news magazine describes the capital punishment question. As recently as 1972, the United States Supreme Court decision in *Furman* v. *Georgia* invalidated existing laws providing for capital punishment. That decision gave new hope to over six hundred convicts in state prisons.

But the tide is turning again. Recent Supreme Court decisions have cleared the way for death sentences under certain conditions, and many states have new laws requiring capital punishment for certain crimes.

In 1977, there were few names better known across America than the name of Gary Gilmore, a man with a tragic past and facing a tragic future. The year began for Gilmore in a death cell in a Utah prison. Gary Gilmore had been condemned to die for murder, but other people had intervened on his behalf.

He himself demanded execution. Often it seemed, however, that he would be given a lighter sentence. On two occasions he tried to kill himself. At last he faced a firing squad, and his long case was closed.

Gilmore's execution was the first since June of 1967. In that month Colorado's gas chamber had been used to put to death Luis Monge for the murder of his wife and three of his ten children. During the intervening decade it seemed that the United States had closed the door on capital punishment for good.

In 1972 the Supreme Court struck down all the nation's death penalty statutes because they placed too much discretion in the hands of judge and jury. The court also voiced the judgment that the death penalty constitutes "cruel and unusual punishment."

Since then the pendulum has slowly swung back the other way. Why? One reason is that in the nine years from 1966 to 1975 the number of murders in the United States nearly doubled, rising from 10,900 in 1966 to more than 20,000 in both 1974 and 1975. Our lawmakers responded. During those nine years, thirty-six states enacted new captial punishment laws.

The Supreme Court modified its 1972 ruling by upholding death penalty laws for murder in three states and rejecting laws in two other states. It rejected statutes automatically imposing death for certain offenses, but approved laws that set standards for guiding juries.

But the real conflict is just starting. *U.S. News and World Report* recently stated, "Arguments over capital punishment are escalating to a feverish pitch." Opponents of the death penalty hope to create a national revulsion against what they see as a form of legalized killing. Others are prepared to battle for capital punishment laws as essential to the survival of our nation.

The issue is a serious one. On the one hand we have a rising tide of violence and death, an appalling disregard for human life. On the other hand, we face the responsibility of taking other lives in retribution.

The Dispute over Capital Punishment

How should Christians view the conflict? Is the death sentence a barbaric relic of the past? Or is it a vital safeguard to the welfare of our country? What does the Bible say on the subject?

The opponents of capital punishment are many and vocal. Abe Fortas, former associate justice of the United States Supreme Court, summed them up in an article entitled "The Case Against Capital Punishment," in *The New York Times Magazine,* January 23, 1978.

"Why," he asks, "when we have bravely and nobly progressed so far in the recent past to create a decent, humane society, must we perpetuate the senseless barbarism of official murder?" Mr. Fortas and those who hold his view point out that at least forty-five nations have abolished capital punishment.

He also underscores the difficulty of administering it fairly. Statistics show that only one out of seventy-five of those guilty of capital punishment crimes are finally brought to execution. And the poor and underprivileged, especially members of racial minorities, are more likely to be executed.

In addition, opponents of the death penalty contend with vigor that capital punishment does not cut down on serious crimes. Life imprisonment, they say, would serve as well.

Many disagree. A growing number of voices are being raised to defend the other side. In fact, a recent Gallup poll showed that 65 percent of those surveyed favored capital punishment. To remove the fear of execution, many believe, will inevitably invite an overwhelming tide of death and violence. To ban capital punishment would constitute another backward step toward permissiveness and anarchy.

Defenders of executions also make the valid point that life sentences in our times are rarely carried out. Many prisoners are too easily paroled. They insist that capital punishment is indeed a deterrent to serious crime.

THE DEMANDS FOR DIVINE JUSTICE

Does God have counsel for us on this subject? He does indeed. In fact, it is only in the light of the Bible that we can hope to find a reasonable and adequate answer. Let us look at the history of capital punishment in the Bible.

Where did capital punishment begin? What we call the death penalty today is virtually as old as the human race. The death penalty began in the times of Noah, when the total population of the world numbered only eight souls. God had destroyed a wicked and violent world civilization. In Genesis 9, we find God setting forth conditions under which human life would make a new beginning. One of His conditions is expressed in verse 6: "Whoso sheddeth man's blood, by man shall his blood be shed: for in the image of God made he man."

Here is the foundation for all human government. At its very base is the imperative for capital punishment. Man was made responsible for enforcing the sanctity of human life. Human life is sacred, not because we are great but because of the greatness of the God whose image we reflect. Notice again Genesis 9:6. "Whoso sheddeth man's blood, by man shall his blood be shed: for in the image of God made he man." The great crime of taking a human life is that we dare to desecrate the image of God. The one who takes a human life destroys something he cannot replace. He cuts off a potential he is powerless to fulfill. And God says the greatest crime of all is that the murderer dares to dishonor Almighty God.

And the human race has reached the place today where man destroys his fellow man without seeming qualm or question. Why? One important reason is that man himself has failed completely to enforce God's demand for capital punishment. There is little doubt that the swift, impartial execution of those found guilty of capital crimes would work to slow down their occurrences.

Let us be careful, however, of saying that God demanded capital punishment primarily as a deterrent. The scripture makes clear that God had a more important reason—the principle of simple justice. Dr. William H. Baker, of the faculty of Moody Bible Institute, has written a scholarly and thoughtful book in which he takes a careful look at what the Bible teaches concerning capital punishment. In *Worthy of Death*, he speaks of retribution, a term that means "the dispensing of reward or punishment according to the deserts of the individual."[1]

He writes, "Retribution is properly a satisfactor or according to the ancient figure of justice and her scales, a restoration of a disturbed equilibrium. As such it is a proper, legitimate and moral concept."[1]

When someone dares to snuff out the divinely given life of another person, he violates a principle of right and wrong as real as the law of gravity. And when God's laws are violated, retribution is demanded.

Strange to say, our so-called enlightened society today has virtually lost sight of the essential fact that ours is a world ruled by a holy God. Many cannot see that He is in control, but He is. Many of God's judgments pass unseen by man. Paul reminds us in 1 Timothy 5:24, "Some men's sins are open beforehand, going before to judgment; and some men they follow after."

God is not being hoodwinked nor is He being overpowered. Broken laws mean retribution. Although man may not fulfill his role, God will, in one way or another.

Some argue, of course, that capital punishment itself expresses irreverence for human life. They even say that to condemn a man to death is to violate the commandment "Thou shalt not kill." A closer look at the meaning of the original Hebrew, however, makes clear that the commandment is, "Thou shalt not commit murder." God is prohibiting individuals from acting in personal anger.

To act administratively in honoring God's law and making sure that it is kept is vastly different from an act of personal vengeance. Paul, speaking in Romans 13, reminds us that administrative power comes from God and acts by his permission. "For he is the minister of God to thee for good," he says in verse 4. "But if thou do that which is evil, be afraid: for he beareth not the sword in vain."

There are also some who say that God's Old Testament law has been rendered obsolete. They argue that Christ taught love and forgiveness. That is an inaccurate understanding of Christ's clear teaching. God is a God of love and compassion, but He is also a God of holiness and justice. Jesus said in Matthew 5:17, "Think not that I am come to destroy the law, or the prophets: I am not come to destroy, but to fulfil."

A little later in the same discourse He spoke specifically of the law that demanded death for death. "Ye have heard that it was said by them of old time," He said, "Though shalt not kill; and whosoever shall kill shall be in danger of the judgment" (Matthew 5:21). The "judgment," of course, is death, but He does not say such a punishment has been or will be suspended. Instead He says that even those angry with another without a reason are in danger of judgment as well.

THE REAL ISSUE OF CAPITAL PUNISHMENT

The issue, very simply, is not whether we need capital punishment for a deterrent to crime, although a case might be made to show that it is indeed a powerful deterrent. And the issue is not whether capital punishment is being administered fairly. If it is not, we need to take steps to assure justice in the fear of God. The real issue is not whether we find the administration of capital punishment comfortable or pleasant. Punishment is never pleasant, but it is needful.

The Christian is concerned *primarily* with obeying the commands of God, a God not of anthropomorphic imagination, but the "High and Holy One" who gives *laws*, not recommendations, requires obedience, not requests cooperation.

We should also remember that capital punishment is, indeed, a deterrent in the sense that *the criminal executed has been effectively deterred* from committing another capital crime.

The issue is whether we will accept or ignore the clear mandate of God. We cannot deny that the world in which we live is steadily growing more violent. In the world and in our nation men are trying to edge God out of the picture.

As a nation, little of what we say or do is based on the Word of God. We have largely rejected God's counsel in government, in business, in schools, and in the family. And we are paying the price.

Will we fail to recognize that God has the first and the last word? We can brush His commands aside, but we must bear the consequences. As Christians, we ought to see the alternatives clearly, pray, and then speak out as those who understand and are committed to the will of God.

NOTES

1. William H. Baker, *Worthy of Death* (Chicago: Moody, 1973), p. 83.

5

Alcohol:
America's Most Costly Luxury

America has many luxuries—large and lavish homes, sleek cars, recreational vehicles by the thousands. But there is something more costly than all those. In terms of total cost—death, sickness, crime, and accident—our greatest national luxury is the use of alcohol.

Some Christians favor the use of alcohol beverages in moderation, whereas other believers insist on total abstinence. Some believe it is possible to drink alcoholic beverages without damaging their Christian testimonies, and others that the only safe rule is total abstinence.

In a recent book titled *Drinking*, Jack B. Weiner brings together a striking series of related tragedies. True stories, these all happened within a few days' time, in places all over the country. The first tragic event took place in Calumet, Oklahoma, several days before Christmas. A nineteen-year-old youth finished drinking a bottle of shaving lotion, then staggered into the corner of an abandoned garage. There, in a drunken stupor, he methodically used a razor blade to slash the artery of his wrist. In thirty minutes he was dead. Later that evening in Denver, Colorado, six hundred miles northwest, a middle-aged woman lapsed into an alcoholic blackout. When she came to, her baby boy had suffocated in his crib.

Still farther north and only hours later, a father of three

children in Great Falls, Montana, choked to death on a three-inch piece of sirloin steak. He had been drinking and failed to cut his steak properly.

The following morning, two thousand miles due east, in Augusta, Maine, a mother and her two young girls were rushed to a hospital for emergency treatment of serious burns. The mother, a widow, had passed out while drinking. Unnoticed, her cigarette dropped down between the cushions of the couch. The blaze that followed almost took three lives. We cannot deny that the world in which we live is steadily growing darker. In the world and in our nation men are trying to edge God out of the picture.

As a nation, little of what we say or do is based on the Word of God. We have largely rejected God's counsel in government, in business, in schools, and in the family. And we are paying the price.

Will we fail to recognize that God has the first and the last word? We can brush His commands aside, but we must bear the consequences. As Christians, we ought to see the alternatives clearly, pray, and then speak out as those who understand and are committed to the will of God.

Although widely scattered, those tragic happenings all had a common cause—the use of alcohol. They are but samples of the tragedies that take place every twenty-four hours of every day across the nation, month after month.[1]

THE REALITY OF THE LIQUOR PROBLEM

From coast to coast, in communities large and small, alcohol leaves destruction in its path. Half of all homicides in the United States and one-third of all suicides are alcohol related.[2] Nearly half the 5.5 million arrests a year in this country involve persons who have used alcohol.

Alcohol is our number one killer on the highways—a factor in some 25,000 deaths and 200,000 injuries each year.[3] Narcotics experts tell us that, notwithstanding marijuana, heroin, and all the rest, alcohol remains the chief drug problem in America.[4] It also constitutes the primary health problem of our nation, a problem that is getting worse.[5]

Researchers at George Washington University say there may be as many as 9 million alcoholics in the United States—nearly one in every twenty persons—plus many millions more on the verge of serious drinking problems. Jack Weiner insists the figure is somewhere between 15 and 20 million.

It is estimated that one out of every ten workers, managers, and executives in the United States suffers from alcoholism.[6] The price tag for lost time, accidents, and related consequences of employee alcoholism has soared to a colossal $15 billion yearly.[7]

Only one thing is more amazing than the ruin left by alcohol, and that is our national unwillingness to get rid of it and free our people from its curse. Statistics tell us that the United States is consuming an annual average of 2.7 gallons of alcoholic beverages for every person fourteen or older in the country. That is no trivial amount. It measures out to 21 fifths of 86-proof whiskey, plus 12.6 fifths of wine, plus 12.5 cases of beer a year for every male and female fourteen years and older in our country.[8]

THE REASONS FOR THE LIQUOR PROBLEM

Why do we permit the misery liquor brings? There seem to be two main reasons. First, some people like the thrills that come with drinking. And nothing—not all its tragedy or cost or misery—can make them give it up. The second reason our nation gives alcohol its unholy place is our insatiable lust for profit. Retail sales of alcoholic beverages for one recent year totaled $32.5 billion. From that our government claimed $9.5 billion in federal, state, and local taxes.[9]

Despite the tragic aftermath of liquor's place in our society, many moral people like to think that the answer to the problem simply lies in moderation. The liquor industry itself joins in this persuasive chorus. "If people would only learn to drink sensibly," they say, "there would be no liquor problem." However, the very nature of alcohol is to weaken the will to drink with moderation.

Recently, in a midwestern Sunday school, a teacher who had been an advocate of drinking in moderation made a startling admission. Only hours before, one of his former public school mates had ended his life by jumping from a twelfth-story hotel window. It was the tragic climax to years of giving in to alcohol. The teacher told the class, "My friend and I thought we could stop. We never dreamed he would become an alcoholic. I think I'm to blame."

Alcohol is no respecter of persons. It could touch you or someone that you love. Once alcoholism picks a victim, prevention is too late.

Observers tell us that although per capita consumption of alcohol has leveled off in recent years, more young people are becoming regular drinkers, and more women are drinking now than in the past.

Meanwhile we are learning that the effects of even moderate drinking can be more serious than we think. Studies recently presented at the quadrennial International Conference on Birth Defects in Montreal give strong indication that even moderate drinking by a pregnant woman—as little as two to four drinks a day—may damage an unborn baby's brain for life.[10]

THE REMEDY FOR THE LIQUOR PROBLEM

In the face of facts like these, what should be the Christian's stand concerning social drinking? Let us remember that one becomes a Christian only by repentance and faith in Jesus Christ, not by any works of righteousness. Faith in Christ makes us new creations with new goals and aims and standards. The Holy Spirit indwells us, and He makes the changes that show that we are Christians.

Some Christians assume that because they have been saved by grace, conduct does not matter. Some even believe that living with a principle of total abstinence constitutes a form of legalism and somehow negates the fact that they have been saved by grace.

But that is a wrong idea of Christian liberty. There is no reason the person saved by grace should not restrict himself to please the Lord who saved him.

The apostle Paul recognized the importance of that principle.

In 1 Corinthians 8, he speaks concerning his right to eat meat that had been offered in heathen temples. In verse 13 he writes, "If meat make my brother to offend, I will eat no flesh while the world standeth."

I see four basic reasons why the Christian should voluntarily abstain from social drinking. First, the Bible suggests that abstinence is a sound position for the earnest Christian. Someone will say at once, "But doesn't the Bible speak of drinking wine? Didn't Jesus drink wine? And the apostle Paul wrote to Timothy, 'Drink no longer water, but use a little wine for thy stomach's sake . . .' " (1 Timothy 5:23). It is interesting that Paul had to urge Timothy to take a *little* wine. That seems to imply that he was not used to taking any wine.

Wine drinking *is* often mentioned in the Bible. However, our English translations make no distinctions between words denoting different kinds of wine. In some cases, especially in the New Testament, the references are to sweet, unfermented wine.

Although the Bible nowhere says one cannot drink wine, it does condemn excess. "Woe unto them that are mighty to drink wine," says Isaiah 5:22, "and men of strength to mingle [or mix] strong drink." Proverbs 20:1 likewise warns, "Wine is a mocker, strong drink is raging: and whosoever is deceived thereby is not wise."

It is interesting to note, however, that God required total abstinence for those in close relationship to Him. Leviticus 10:9 forbids the use of wine to priests who ministered in the Tabernacle. Wine was likewise forbidden to those under special vows to God as Nazarites (Numbers 6:3).

Should the New Testament believer be less holy than those separated to God in Old Testament times? Peter writes, "But as he which hath called you is holy, so be ye holy in all manner of conversation; because it is written, Be ye holy; for I am holy" (1 Peter 1:15-16).

Paul writes, "Let us walk honestly [or decently], as in the day; not in rioting and drunkenness, not in chambering and wantonness. . . . But put ye on the Lord Jesus Christ, and make no provision for the flesh, to fulfill the lusts thereof" (Romans 13:13-14).

But some will say, "Did not the Lord Jesus Christ turn water into wine?" He did, indeed. One must remember, of course, that He was providing the accepted refreshment of the day.

Although Bible scholars differ, there is no absolute evidence that the wine He made had intoxicating qualities. The narrative in John 2 makes a point that the wine He made was distinctive in its taste, clearly different from that provided earlier by the hosts. In this, our Lord's first miracle, illustrating the newness of the life He gives, it is debatable that Jesus would provide a wine that would intoxicate.

A second reason for abstinence is the role and character of alcohol in our modern world. Liquor today, especially in our country, is the partner of excess and evil. Overall, the brewing, sale, and distribution of liquor is a monstrous evil in which no Christian should want to have a part.

One cannot drink without giving endorsement to a baneful custom and a conscienceless enterprise. It is unthinkable that a Christian should contribute to an industry that deals in death, misery, and the ruin of countless lives. A very pointed command is given in 1 Thessalonians 5:22: "Abstain from all appearance of evil," or "from every form of evil." One cannot argue that drinking is a harmless custom when millions are alcoholics.

What are the present-day associations of alcohol? Can we find any that are good or uplifting or honoring to God? Social drinking is at best a "detente" with the god that holds millions in bondage. And, as Paul asks, "What fellowship hath righteousness with unrighteousness? and what communion hath righteousness with unrighteousness? and what concord hath Christ with Belial?" (2 Corinthians 6:14-15).

A third reason for abstinence is that drinking, even in moderation, can be destructive to one's personal Christian life. Alcohol is harmful to the body. The great inventor Thomas Edison said, "To put alcohol in the body is like putting sand on the bearings of an engine. It doesn't belong." Centuries earlier,

William Shakespeare spelled out the same essential truth when he wrote, "Alcohol is a poison men take into the mouth to steal away the brain."

Medical research is showing that alcohol not only has an immediate, short-range effect but also inevitably brings about long-range damage to the human system. Brain cells die when alcohol is taken into the bloodstream. Heart, liver, and kidneys are also permanently affected. If you are a Christian, your body is the temple of the Holy Spirit. You should not defile or damage it by subjecting it to liquor.

Not only is alcohol detrimental to the body, it also is spiritually and morally degrading. Even moderate drinking cannot but fog the mind and cloud the spirit.

Finally, a Christian should abstain for the sake of others, especially those who may be influenced by his example. Experience shows that for every dozen people who choose the path of social drinking, one will become an alcoholic before ten years have passed. Three others will teeter on the brink, becoming problem drinkers.[11] Eight out of every dozen social drinkers succeed as moderate drinkers, but four others will fail, and one of them will drop off the precipice of addiction. There is no telling which ones will be affected.

In the light of such facts, Romans 14:21 speaks to us pointedly. "It is good neither to eat flesh, nor drink wine, nor anything whereby thy brother stumbleth, or is offended, or is made weak."

Your decision on this issue is crucial. There are no signs that our national alcohol problem is getting better. It is getting worse. Not only men and women, but children and youth are deeply affected. The liquor industry aims to bring its products into every home and family in the United States. Estimates indicate that American breweries, wineries, and distilleries will spend from $500 million to 1 billion dollars in advertising this year. Government and business, by and large, are sympathetic to the liquor industry.

It seems clear that the only safe principle for a Christian is total abstinence from alcoholic beverages in any form. In light of the cost, in terms of lives, property, and health, alcohol is a luxury we cannot afford.

NOTES

1. Jack B. Weiner, *Drinking* (New York: Norton, 1976), pp. 2-3.
2. Ibid., p. 3.
3. *Christianity Today,* 6 November 1970, p. 28.
4. "Drinking Plateau Reached?" *The American Issue,* January-February 1977, p. 3.
5. *Christianity Today,* p.28.
6. Weiner, p. 42.
7. Ibid., p. 41.
8. "Drinking Plateau Reached?" *The American Issue,* p.3.
9. *Reader's Digest,* February 1977, p. 163.
10. Joan Beck, "Even Social Drinking by a Woman Can Harm a Fetus," *The Chicago Tribune,* 26 August 1977.
11. Walter S. Krusich, "Alcohol: Headache Around the World," *Moody Monthly,* December 1972.

6

The Question of Civil Disobedience

Verdict: *Peter and John, guilty of civil disobedience.* These unauthorized preachers, after healing a lame man, stirred the people by attributing the miracle to Jesus Christ and by proclaiming the resurrection. Furthermore, Peter boldly accused the religious leaders of being responsible for the crucifixion of Jesus Christ. For such crimes Peter and John were sentenced to jail.

Verdict: *John Bunyan, guilty of civil disobedience.* The author of *Pilgrim's Progress* failed to attend the Church of England and persisted in preaching without proper credentials. Therefore, he was found guilty of breaking the king's laws. Arrested three times, Bunyan spent thirteen years in jail for such crimes.

Verdict: *Martin Niemöller guilty of civil disobedience.* During World War II, this German pastor stood before Hilter and declared, "God is my Führer." For this crime he was removed from his pulpit and placed in a concentration camp.

THE APOSTLES AND CIVIL DISOBEDIENCE

The issue of civil disobedience is not new. For centuries Christians have been caught between giving their allegiance to God and obeying the laws of man. Ever since A.D. 30, when the Jerusalem hierarchy desperately tried to silence Peter and John (Acts 5), Christians occasionally have been forced to disobey some of man's orders. Peter and John refused to be silent in the face of a threatened jail sentence. These first preachers of the gospel had received their authority from Jesus Christ Himself; but because they lacked the necessary papers and approval from the authorities of their day, the Jerusalem leaders were determined to stop them. They thought Peter and John were too irregular. They did not fit the established order of the day; they were transformed nonconformists.

The priests in charge of the Temple were disturbed by these men because the priests desired things to be done in a certain way. Money changers selling their doves were allowed, but children of God lifting their voices in unrehearsed praise were out of order. The Sadducees, one sect of religious leaders, did not believe in a resurrection, and they were determined to stop anyone preaching about the subject. And miracles were stirring people up. All this was dreadfully irregular.

The apostles were arrested late at night. The authorities knew that if they made their arrest during daylight hours, the public might protest. So they were careful to carry out their challenge of God's Word under cover of darkness.

But the Word of God cannot be bound. The apostles had unquestionable power behind them. It must have dismayed the authorities that the evidence was so incontrovertible. When the lame man stood before them whole, they could not deny that power.

What made the disobedience of the apostles legitimate? Supernatural power caused them to speak. And that same kind of supernatural power should characterize every Christian. The work of the church is ministering to people. We are to find people who are lying at the gate, excluded from our worship; to lift them up; and to make them worshipers of Jesus Christ. The church will convince no one of its right to speak unless it can point to changed lives in men and women. The world wants to see miracles.

Another thing that upset the authorities was the apostles' persistence. The hierarchy was used to seeing people melt in their presence. Those priests even bent the Roman officials to their wills. But the simple boldness of the apostles was shocking. There was only one way to stop them—forbid them by law to preach. Then if they persisted, they could be jailed.

But the religious leaders forgot that the believers lived by a higher authority. Said Peter, "We ought to obey God rather than men." When civil law opposes God's clear commandments, we are obliged to obey God. There are times when it is right to disobey the laws of men.

THE BIBLE AND CIVIL DISOBEDIENCE

But there are also times when it is wrong to disobey human authority. A few more examples from the Scripture will illustrate the distinction.

Exodus 1 tells of an Egyptian ruler who ordered the death of every Hebrew male child. Verse 17 says, "But the midwives feared God, and did not as the king of Egypt commanded them." Jochebed, the mother of Moses, engaged in civil disobedience when she hid her child in a basket among the reeds in the river. Hers was not mere rebellion, however; it was obedience to the will of God.

Consider Daniel 6 and the law of Darius that "whosoever shall ask a petition of any God or man for thirty days . . . he shall be cast into the den of lions." Daniel, fully aware of the law, disobeyed it. Daniel "went into his house . . . and prayed and gave thanks before his God, as he did aforetime" (Daniel 6:10). Daniel too disobeyed the king's law. But his desire was not to express rebellion—it was to be in conformity with God's clearly revealed will.

Jeremiah criticized the government of his time so severely that he was jailed and called a traitor to his nation. But the substance of his criticism was the Word of God. He was not motivated by a desire just to disobey.

What is the other side to the question? The Scriptures speak clearly concerning the Christian's responsibility to obey his government. First Peter 2:13 tells us, "Submit yourselves to every ordinance of man for the Lord's sake: whether it be to the king, as supreme." "Let every soul be subject unto the higher powers. For there is no power but of God: the powers that be are ordained of God" (Romans 13:1). Peter and Paul are saying that no civil power exists except by God's permission. Therefore, whoever resists civil power resists God's ordinance, unless the civil power demands disobedience to a clear commandment of God's Word.

The story of the rebellion of Korah and a band of Israelites is found in Numbers 16. The government of the day was a theocracy, and Moses was God's chosen civil leader. When the people rebelled against the authority of Moses, God judged them with sudden death, because Moses, the civil leader, represented God's authority. A rebellion against him constituted a rebellion against God.

Now, of course, the problem is to reconcile what may be apparently contradictory instructions of Scripture. On the one hand, we are to view the authority of civil government as God-given authority. On the other hand, we are not to obey any civil laws that contradict God's Word. That is a difficult problem to many Christians today.

THE CHRISTIAN AND CIVIL DISOBEDIENCE

Here are conflicts some of our brothers and sisters in Christ have faced in recent years:

Christians in China during the communist takeover suddenly found themselves under a law that forbade them to gather for religious services. Yet the Bible commanded them not to forsake the assembling of themselves together.

A family of Christians living in Germany during Hitler's time had to decide whether to turn over Jewish neighbors to the secret police, or defy the government and hide them.

A pastor in Russia was given the choice of jail if he continued to preach against the atheistic doctrines of Communism, or freedom if he would merely teach the sections of Scripture that would not conflict.

A believer in Christ living in Cuba had to decide whether he would join a revolutionary movement to overthrow the godless government of Fidel Castro.

A young Christian, a citizen of the United States, believed that his country was involved in an unjust war. He was being drafted, and others encouraged him to resist the draft because of his moral convictions.

Some guidelines in deciding what to do in difficult situations like those should help us.

First, disobedience, if necessary, must be without violence. To be violent or to hurt someone is contrary to the teaching of the Word of God. The riots that shake our country are violent and evil. Such demonstrations are perpetrated by extremists who have no use for the laws of God.

Second, the law being disobeyed must be clearly contrary to the Word of God. We cannot disobey merely as a matter of preference. Peter and John are examples. They were commanded by their Lord to bear witness to the things they had seen and heard. The command of the authorities to be silent was clearly in conflict with God's word to them.

Many young men who have resisted the draft in recent years have disobeyed simply because they feel no obligation to serve their country. But others believe God's Word specifically teaches that Christians should resist military service. Their stance as conscientious objectors is a matter of genuine conviction. Each young person must decide these matters in light of the Spirit's teaching in the Word of God. And the laws of the United States provide for honest, conscientious objectors.

Third, disobedience must not be a general rebellion against civil government as a whole, because all governments (both good ones and bad ones) fall within God's permissive and directive will. Peter and Paul lived and served while wicked Nero held sway, yet both commanded believers to be submissive to the government. The direct teaching of Scripture requires respect and submission to government (Romans 13:1-7; 1 Peter 2:13-17).

Henry David Thoreau wrote, "It is not desirable to cultivate a respect for the law, so much as for the right." But, we must ask, who decides what is right? The government may make a mistake, but so may the people. If seven people disobey, that is one thing. But if seven million disobey, that is anarchy.

Finally, Christians must be willing to bear the consequences of disobedience to civil authority. Peter and John were so committed to Jesus Christ that they were willing to suffer ridicule, jail, and death to get out the gospel. They willingly accepted the punishment that resulted from their disobedience.

The Scriptures are clear that ordinarily the commandments of God and the commandments of government are not in conflict. They also establish that God is the Lord of the Christian's conscience. However, for the most part, obedience is in and disobedience is out. If we are forbidden to bear witness to salvation in Christ, we must disobey that command. If we are ordered by authorities to do evil in the sight of God, we must disobey.

But there is much that can be done without disobeying! Christians in the United States are blessed with freedom and possibly more governmental tolerance than any other nation in history. Our government was established with freedom of religion as one of its fundamental principles, and we still largely enjoy that freedom.

One of the greatest threats to today's church is that it will get sucked into the spirit of rebellion that seems to prevail in our age. Already some formerly sound religious groups have become major exponents of worldwide revolution. There is nothing that resembles such rebellion and arrogance in the teachings of Christ or in the example of the early church.

Civil disobedience is sometimes called for. Those occasions are rare, and it must be done humbly, prayerfully, and wisely, in accordance with God's Word.

7

The Christian School Versus the Public School

Today there is a fresh, new breeze in the troubled world of education. And it is coming from the Christian school. In a day when most educators are worried, Christian schools are showing vigor and new promise.

Even the prestigious *Wall Street Journal* recognizes that. Recently, sandwiched in with columns of stock quotations and national and business news, was a report from Southern Pines, North Carolina.

Because the teaching in the schools was inferior and conflicted with pupil's religious beliefs, some parents from Calvary Christian Church pulled their children out of the public school system. Their congregation built its own school. Christianity and the basic skills of reading, writing, and arithmetic are being taught by the school's twelve teachers and learned by its student body of 125 pupils.[1]

The report continues for more than a full column. It notes that the number of Christian schools is steadily growing. One estimate places the number of interdenominational Christian schools at 5,000. By 1990 Christian schools will outnumber public schools if current growth trends continue.[2] A specialist with the United States Office of Education says that Christian schools are the fastest growing segment in private education today.[3]

Why have Christian leaders and parents across the land chosen to enter the field of education? There is a price to pay, of course. Each new Christian school involves a tremendous cost in terms of study, prayer, personal sacrifice, and money. The answer is the growing concern of thoughtful Christian parents for the course of public education. The secular outlook in schools today, they believe, demands an alternative for Christians.

I do not want to be misunderstood. We live in a day when the American public is all too prone to condemn and criticize. There are thousands of conscientious and dedicated people deeply involved in our public schools. Among them are many dedicated Christians. They deserve our thanks and appreciation for their important contributions. However, trends in the field of education are such that the Christian parent must at least consider the possibilities of a Christian education. Let me suggest four issues to be considered in regard to the question.

The Directive: Parents Are Responsible for Education

Who is responsible for the task of education? The Bible clearly says God assigned that job to parents. Speaking of His commandments, God says in Deuteronomy 6:7, "And thou shalt teach them diligently unto thy children, and shalt talk of them when thou sittest in thine house, and when thou walkest by the way, and when thou liest down, and when thou risest up." If God has given you children, your task will not be complete until they have the best and most adequate preparation to meet the tests of life. We dare not casually pass along our task to others, without being certain what they are teaching our children.

Send your child to school today, and by the time he receives his high school diploma you will have delegated 16,000 hours of time to outside teachers. At the very least, you need to be concerned about how all those hours are used.

The Disappointment: Public Schools Are Failing

Deuteronomy 6 tells us that the prime concern of education should be not the skills of life, important as they are, but a grounding in the fear and knowledge of God. Secular education writes off that obligation completely.

Education without God tends merely to teach the young how to make a living. It teaches them culture and the arts as a means of enjoying life, but it does not teach them wisdom. It does not teach them how to make vital life decisions.

A study of education will clearly show that educators through the centuries have taught succeeding generations to be man-centered. God, for the most part, has been forgotten and even opposed. That is especially true today. In 1963, the Supreme Court ruled that Bible reading and prayer in the public schools are not constitutional. The ruling then was new, but the spirit behind it was not. For centuries we have been moving down the road toward excluding God and the Bible from public education.

The most serious effect of the 1963 decision is not that it cuts off children from prayer and Bible reading. Prayer and Bible reading can and should be done at home. Rather, the ruling says, in a way no young person can misunderstand, that God and faith have no essential place in education.

Surely that is one of the most basic points of failure in our public education system. It shouts that faith in God and reliance in the Bible are add-ons in the process of education. They are not really needed.

That is one reason for the growing number of Christian schools. Many parents believe that God should not be barred from education. But there are other reasons. One is the parent reaction to the rising tide of violence in our public schools. Violence in the schools has more than tripled in this decade. Some 70,000 teachers are physically assaulted in schools each year, not to mention assaults of students.[4] Parents naturally fear for the safety of their children. But beyond all that, they know that schools today are schools of lawlessness, permissiveness, and often violence.

There is a growing feeling that our secular schools are failing in their basic job of teaching the essentials. Each year taxpayers foot an education bill in excess of $144 billion, then watch helplessly as Scholastic Aptitude Test scores plummet.[5]

For all our national stress on education, surveys from time to time show distressing percentages of the functionally illiterate. Colleges complain that high school graduates come to them inadequately prepared to read and write. Average scores for Scholastic Aptitude Tests in math are down 10 percent from fifteen years ago. School effectiveness varies greatly, of course. But many parents have taken their children from public schools to place them in Christian institutions because of disappointment in the learning situation. In a report for the Center for the Study of Democratic Institutions, Dr. Robert M. Hutchins charges that our education institutions are not imparting "the arts of reading writing, speaking, listening and figuring."

The content of what public education is teaching also troubles many thoughtful Christians. Pupils are not only subjected to teaching that excludes faith in God and the Bible, but they are indoctrinated in what one Christian educator calls the "deadly duo" of evolution and humanism.

Dr. Paul A. Kienel, executive director of the Association of Christian Schools International, lists eight significant humanistic assumptions inherent today in our public education:

1. Man is supreme. If this is true, there is no higher power.
2. Man evolved from lower forms of life. Consequently, there was no act of divine creation.
3. Man is an animal. Therefore, he cannot have a soul.
4. Man is inherently good. He does not need a Savior.
5. Common practice sets the standard. This, of course, is the assumption that whatever the majority does, must be the thing to do. If this is true, there are no moral absolutes.
6. Criminals are merely antisocial. The implication here is that lawbreakers have a problem, but they are not really sinners.
7. The term maladjustment explains all adverse human behavior. In other words, there is no such thing as guilt.
8. Finally, secular education assumes that bad environment is to blame for evil. If this is true, man himself is not responsible.[6]

Those are assumptions interwoven in every facet of secular

education—in English and literature, in government and sociology, in biology and general science. They are transmitted not only in textbooks, but also by the personal views of the majority of teachers, who were trained and indoctrinated in secular institutions where humanism reigns.

Christian parents object to specific teachings of certain textbooks—books that have socialistic and communistic viewpoints. They object to salacious literature. Parents can protest, of course, but as a minority their voice is seldom heard.

THE DIRECTIVE: A COMPLETE BIBLICAL EDUCATION

Those are some of the many reasons Christian parents especially are turning away from secular education today. And there are equally important reasons they are finding Christian schools effective. Let me first of all dispel an illusion. Often the public assumes that Christian schools give all their time to teaching the Bible itself. That is not true.

Christian schools are schools, not Sunday schools or Bible classes, although the Bible is read and often memorized. Pupils and teachers pray. They study and relate as Christians. Pupils focus on the familiar basic subjects. They learn reading, math, writing, history, science, and other subjects required for college preparation. They meet prescribed basic educational standards.

In general, Christian schools tend toward fewer frills than our secular education system—fewer courses that border on the hobby level and far-out lines of specialization. Extracurricular activities are more limited; pupils give more time to serious learning.

This may explain, for example, the record set recently by eighth graders enrolled in schools affiliated with the Association of Christian Schools International. These students in 1,200 member schools scored twelve months above the national average on the Stanford Achievement Test.[7]

Although the situation may vary from school to school, many parents believe their children are getting better teaching in Christian schools than in the public system. Discipline is better maintained; children learn respect for the law and order. They learn to work and study. Classes tend to be smaller than in public schools, so children receive more personal attention. The *Wall Street Journal* quotes Perry King, a biology teacher at a Christian school in North Carolina. "I have ten students in my biology class," he says. "I can give them as much attention as they need. I can discipline them if I need to. If they don't learn in this situation, we just don't have an excuse."[8]

Christian schools must meet state standards for teachers. Teachers often have to teach more subjects and are usually paid less than teachers in the public schools. But more of those who teach in Christian classrooms are there because they want to serve.

The great distinctive of Christian schools, however, lies in their overall approach to education. God is not ignored but is made the center of all learning. Children are taught to make important judgments, to choose the right, and reject the wrong. The Christian school attempts to turn the searchlight of the Scriptures on every aspect of education. The Bible becomes a guide for discerning truth, a help in choosing what is good.

History, geography, science, social studies, and all the rest are presented in the light of Bible teaching. Most Christian schools do not ignore the theory of evolution, but they study it as a theory, not as a fact. They learn to see its fallacies. They see the wonder and meaning of creation.

The place of the Bible in this kind of Christian school is the same as the place of the Bible in the Christian life. It is a discerner, a yardstick, an evaluator. Psalm 119:105 says, "Thy Word is a lamp unto my feet, and a light unto my path." Hebrews 4:12 says, "The word of God is quick and powerful, and sharper than any two-edged sword, piercing even to the dividing asunder of soul and spirit."

Secular education has laid the Bible aside—even banned the Bible—and is walking in the dark. Christian schools are setting education on its feet by restoring the Bible to its proper place.

THE DOUBT: DO CHRISTIAN SCHOOLS ISOLATE CHILDREN?

Some people say that Christian schools are fine—but. And one of the biggest objections they raise is the charge of isolation. Christian schools, they say, shut up children in an unreal world. They will emerge as hothouse plants, unable to cope with the secular world in which they have to live.

But that is a weak objection. Students at Christian schools do not enter a monastery. They live and play with non-Christian children in their neighborhoods, meet others on the streets and at places of recreation. They watch television and listen to the radio. Inevitably they read comics, see the same magazines, and come under many of the same influences as students in secular schools.

Meanwhile, their teachers in their Christian schools are realistic people. Their concern above all, is to help their pupils cope with the world as they will find it. Dr. Roy W. Lowrie, Jr. writes in a pamphlet on this subject, "The Christian school does shelter students. It shelters them from the prevalence of drugs, lack of discipline, sexual promiscuity, situational ethics, disrespect for authority, drinking, occultism, atheism and agnostic values.

"[But] as a professional educator, and . . . a father, I earnestly believe that kind of sheltering . . . is highly desirable."[9] With that I thoroughly agree.

Christian schools—well-conducted Christian schools—are friends of Christian parents today. Christian schools provide the kind of education that the Bible says our children need. If you are not already involved in a Christian school situation, perhaps it is time at least to investigate.

What kind of education are your children getting? What kind of textbooks are they studying? What kind of teachers shape them for tomorrow? Do you know?

NOTES

1. *Wall Street Journal,* 7 December 1978.
2. Dave Raney, "Public School vs. Christian School," *Moody Monthly,* September 1978, p. 44.

3. *Wall Street Journal,* 7 December 1978.
4. Raney, p. 44.
5. Ibid.
6. Paul L. Kienel, "Do Christian Schools Care About Discipline," *Christian School Comment,* April 1973. Used by permission.
7. *Wall Street Journal,* 7 December 1978.
8. Ibid.
9. Roy W. Lowrie, Jr., "Are Christian Students Too Sheltered?" Pamphlet. Christian Schools Today, 464 Main Road, Newton Square, PA 19073.

8

The Problem of Homosexuality

The most explosive issues of our day are those that have their roots in human rights—the right to basic freedom, the right to education, the right to work, the right to worship as I may feel led. But should I have the right to do something you are convinced is morally wrong?

That is the crux of what is called the "gay rights" issue. Across the land, pressure is increasing to give homosexuals access to jobs of every kind, the right to be accepted as foster parents, and even the right to marry each other. Beneath it all is the insistence that the public change its thinking about the validity of the homosexual pattern.

THE CONFLICT OF HOMOSEXUALITY

A forty-year-old mother from Dallas believes she is a victim of discrimination. She is divorced but wants custody of her eleven-year-old son. A few years ago, a jury decided against her because she is a homosexual, living with a woman companion.

Gay organizations and the National Organization for Women came to her defense. Her newly published book is being filmed for television as a network movie. Meanwhile the mother and her living companion are traveling around the country raising funds for legal appeals.

She says, "They didn't prove I was an unfit mother. The issues are the right to privacy, due process, and the separation of church and state. I'm a very Christian person, but I learned in eighth grade civics that laws aren't supposed to be based on the Bible."[1]

Can a person be a good parent and still be a homosexual? Can a homosexual be a Christian? What should be our attitude as Christians toward the homosexual life-style? Equally important, what should be our attitude toward persons in the grip of homosexual practices? What does the Bible have to say about the issue?

More and more we are hearing about the issue of gay rights. Only a few years ago Anita Bryant was projected into national prominence—condemned by some and praised by others—for her successful efforts in opposing a gay rights ordinance in Dade County, Florida.

Twenty years ago a discussion of homosexual rights in our society would have been unthinkable. Today, however, the pros and cons of gay acceptance are very much an issue. Many people—including some who say they are Christians—accept homosexuality as a legitimate alternative life-style. In the next few months and years the country will be obliged to make decisions on many of these issues.

A great deal of uncertainty is evident. Some time ago, *Time* magazine in an essay "The Homosexual in America" made this discerning comment:

> Beset by inner conflicts, the homosexual is unsure of his own position in society. . . . A vast majority of people retain a deep loathing toward him, but there is a growing mixture of tolerance, empathy or apathy.[2]

Society is torn between condemnation of the homosexual and compassion for him, the article continued. The deviate's plea is that he be treated just like everybody else, yet it is known that he is not like everybody else.[3]

In simple terms, a homosexual is one evidencing sexual desire toward a member of the same sex, men with men or women with women. It may express itself merely in preference for intimate companionship. More often it involves a sexual act. Psychologists tell us that one may yield to homosexual tendencies occasionally or often. Others may follow the homosexual pattern for all or most of their lives.

The first question to be faced is whether homosexuality is wrong, as most of us have been instructed. The answer, quite simply and on the authority of God's Word is—yes, it is.

The big push of homosexuality today is to defend its practices as just another life-style. To buttress that position, homosexuals offer an amazing array of arguments. They say that homosexuals are born with their sexual preferences, just as others are born with heterosexual preferences. They cite the fact that sodomy is widespread, even common, and that when carried on in private it is no one's business but their own. They argue that other kinds of sexual indulgences are condoned or overlooked. In fact, within the past dozen or fifteen years the whole emphasis of homosexuals has been to defend the validity of their practice and press for what they call "gay rights."

Says one psychiatrist, "It is clear that it is becoming increasingly unpopular in the movement to ask or be asked the old question, 'Why are we what we are?' The trend is, unmistakably, to reject this question as arbitrarily posed, very possibly unanswerable, and most important of all, immaterial."[4]

The same authority goes on to say, "The homosexual is coming more and more to regard himself as in no way inferior because of his homosexuality, or homosexuality as in no way inferior to its counterpart as a valid mode of human self-expression; and he is expecting that society will eventually come around to a similar view."[5]

Today homosexuals are highly organized, having a network of regional conferences and a national clearinghouse to facilitate exchange of information. A national legal defense fund exists, and lawyers are instantly available to press the battle for gay rights wherever a need arises.

THE CONFUSION OF HOMOSEXUALITY

In all this, the Bible inevitably has come under sharp attack. Some homosexuals say the Bible should have no place in setting moral standards. Others seek to show by Scripture that the Bible itself justifies the homosexual life-style.

No Christian should be deceived. The Bible clearly tells us that homosexuality is without defense. Genesis 19 describes the homosexual lusts of the men of Sodom, which led to destruction of that city.

Homosexuals cite Ezekiel 16:49, which mentions Sodom's other sins—"pride, fulness of bread, and abundance of idleness," as well as failure to help the poor and needy, but forget that the next verse goes on to say, "and they . . . committed abomination before me; therefore I took them away." So clearly is Sodom's destruction linked with the practice of homosexuality that the term *sodomy* today still has a single meaning.

The Levitical law expresses God's principles of righteousness. Here, in Leviticus 18:22, God's commandment says, "Thou shalt not lie with mankind as with womankind; it is abomination." The fact that that is followed by a commandment against sexual acts with animals suggests the unthinkable nature of the homosexual relation.

There are other prohibitions in the Bible against homosexuality. One of the most revealing New Testament statements is in Romans 1, which tells how men once knew Almighty God, but turned from Him to idols. The passage goes on to say that because men gave up God, God in turn gave up men to "uncleanness through the lusts of their own hearts, to dishonor their own bodies between themselves."

Could this be homosexuality? The following verses make the fact too clear to miss. "For this cause God gave them up unto vile affections; for even their women did change the natural use into that which is against nature; and likewise also the men, leaving the natural use of the woman, burned in their lust one toward another, men with men, working that which is unseemly" (Romans 1:24, 26-27).

Does that mean that homosexuality is a curse on especially godless men? That is not what the Bible is saying. Paul *is* saying that homosexuality was brought into the race because man turned from God. It is one of many sins—and others are enumerated in the closing verses of the same chapter.

Homosexuality, like alcoholism, cursing, or violence, gets its hold on an individual in many different ways. The only ultimate solution is the blood of Jesus Christ.

If homosexuality is sin, then man is ultimately responsible, not just for the sin but for rejecting deliverance from that sin through faith in Jesus Christ. And that is what the New Testament says in 1 Corinthians 6:9-10.

"Do you not know that the unrighteous shall not inherit the kingdom of God? Do not be deceived; neither fornicators, nor idolaters, nor adulterers, nor effeminate, nor homosexuals, nor thieves, nor the covetous, nor drunkards, nor revilers, nor swindlers shall inherit the kingdom of God" (NASB*).

Homosexuality is a serious and offensive sin. But by far its worst effect is that it, along with other sins, can keep a man or woman outside of heaven forever. Today there are millions of homosexuals in our country—some believe as many as 20 million. The degrading effect is beyond our understanding. But the tragedy above all else is that they are letting their lust come between them and the blessing of salvation.

Genesis 4 tells how the world's first murderer, Cain, turned his back on God and occupied himself with other things. He built a city. He had a family. Soon his descendants were wrapped up in making a go of life without the help of God. They developed ranching interests. Some became musicians. One became a skillful metal worker. They built a great society, but they built it without God.

There is not much doubt that numbers of homosexuals today will go on building a society of their own. They may even get what they call "gay rights." But it will be a society walled off from God.

THE CURE FOR HOMOSEXUALITY

Let us be careful of our thinking, however. There is a remedy for homosexuality, and God has put it in our hands. After

---

New American Standard Bible.

declaring in 1 Corinthians 6:9-10 that no homosexual can inherit the kingdom of God, Paul goes on to say in verse 11, "And such were some of you: but ye are washed, but ye are sanctified, but ye are justified in the name of the Lord Jesus, and by the Spirit of our God."

What is this saying? The Word of God is telling us that although no one can hang on to homosexuality and still be accepted by Almighty God, some former homosexuals in the church at Corinth had found deliverance. They had entered a brand new life by faith in Jesus Christ.

We must be careful however about thinking that we can merely tell a homosexual to get right with God and expect him to become a Christian. Homosexual desire grips the heart and life with a strength and fury beyond anything most of us have ever experienced. Much love and prayer and concern are always needed. Much patience, too, and possibly much counseling. But the power of Jesus Christ does have the ultimate answer.

Is our attitude toward homosexuals really representative of Christ? Can we find the grace to love the sinner while we abhor the sin? Can we accept the person, yet keep from giving ground to desires and practices that are evil?

I believe in certain rights for homosexuals. They have the same rights as other men and women bearing an awesome weight of sin to share in the power of the gospel.

William Barclay writes, "The proof of Christianity [in Corinth] lay in its power. It could take the dregs of humanity and make men out of them. It could take men lost to shame and make them sons of God. . . . No man can change himself, but Christ can change him."

The church today is in the world at a time of desperate need. We must resist the adversary, but we must hold out the hope of life and deliverance through Christ to those who will be lost without it.

NOTES

1. "A Lesbian Mother Still Fights to Regain Custody of Her Son," *Chicago Daily News,* 10 August 1977.
2. *Time,* 21 January 1966, pp. 40-41.
3. Ibid.
4. Foster Gunnison, "An Introduction to the Homophile Movement." Pamphlet. (N.p., 1967), p. 28.
5. Ibid., p. 29.
6. William Barclay, "The Daily Study Bible," *The Letters to the Corinthians* (Philadelphia: Westminster, 1956), p. 60.

9

The Unseen Faces of Communism

What philosophy of government has risen to power in our twentieth century by consistently deceiving its citizens? What system was the first to use hostages as weapons against its enemies? What political party has in less than a century mushroomed from a mere handful of loyal supporters to a worldwide movement?

The answer to those questions is one word—Communism. Communism deceives. Communism oppresses. Communism marches beneath the banner of an empty hope. Yet the shadow of Communism falls on half of our world at this moment. What should we know about Communism?

Seven Russians and their families will always remember April 27, 1979. On that date, five Soviet dissidents, all of them under sentence in Russian labor camps, arrived in Kennedy International Airport in New York to begin life as free men. A few hours later, two convicted Russian spies, each under sentence for buying United States military secrets, were put on a plane bound for Moscow. The Russian spies were released in exchange for the freedom of the five.

Among those given their freedom in the exchange were Ukrainian Baptist pastor Georgi Vins and human rights activist Alexander Ginsburg. What a strange exchange! Two convicted spies for the freedom of five of that country's citizens—men who wanted to leave.

Something is seriously wrong in a country where passports for dissidents must be purchased by exchanging them for spies. Something is wrong when refugees must by the thousands stream from countries that boast of the people's rights. And yet every year new countries pick up the communist banner. "Liberation" is their cry. "We want a people's government!"

THE DOMINATION OF COMMUNISM

From the standpoint of growth, Communism is a success. In three-quarters of a century, Communism has grown from nothing at all to become a system that controls the lives and fortunes of more than 1.5 billion people.

The movement began at the turn of this present century when Vladimir Ilyich Lenin established the movement known as Bolshevism in Russia. In 1903 the movement had only seventeen supporters. In 1917 Lenin was able to take control of Russia's millions with only 40,000 in his party. By 1928 there were forty-six communist parties with 1.6 million members. Today there are more than one hundred different parties with a total membership of 60 million people.

In recent years, two things have happened. First, there has been a Communism explosion! More and more countries have joined the communist block of nations. Second, Communism has become a many-sided movement. Whereas once the Soviet Union was the undisputed model of the communist state, Communism now seems to follow a number of different patterns. The Soviet Union is at odds with China. Eastern European countries like Yugoslavia have made clear that they want to forge their own communist regimes. In other countries, like Spain and Italy, Communists are content to carry on as one of several political parties.

The apparent fragmentation puzzles many in the West. Is the communist movement breaking up? Is this a hopeful sign? The best answer seems to be that although Communists want independence from one another, they have a common aim—the conquest of the world. Aleksandr Solzhenitsyn bluntly states that a nation's very life is often destroyed so that Communism can implement its ideals. Chinese Communism is no better than the Soviet variety. To think for a moment that relief is actually reaching the starving people of Cambodia is naive. The army and government of the Heng Samrin regime are receiving all the benefits.[1]

Few non-Communists today really understand Communism. They assume that Communism involves government ownership of land and factories, but in other ways, communist thinking is like our own.

That is not the case!

THE DOCTRINES OF COMMUNISM

An Australian doctor, Dr. Fred Schwarz, was stunned by the tactics of the Communists in his homeland years ago. As a result, he began an intensive study of Communism and for more than twenty years has headed the Christian Anti-Communist Crusade in Long Beach, California. Today he is still interpreting Communism and pointing out basic facts that everyone should know.

Keep in mind that the Communism we know today is a fusion of the thinking of German philospher Karl Marx and the organizing genius of Russian leader Vladimir Ilyich Lenin. Every committed Communist today in Russia, China, Vietnam, or Africa claims to be a Marxist-Leninist. What do Marxist-Leninists believe?

First, they believe that society around the world is engaged in a great ongoing struggle. It is not a conflict between nations, between right or wrong, or between God and Satan, but between the interests of two classes of people. One class is made up of those who get their wealth by owning and managing property. The other is the class that makes a living by hiring out as laborers.

Communists believe that if you are born in the owner-manager class, you will have one set of principles and instincts, and they will never change. Or, if you are a member of the worker class—the *Proletariat,* they call it—you will have a different set of qualities. Marxists are convinced that the property-owning class has its heart set on bigger profits. Workers they say, on the other hand, struggle for the highest possible wage.

As Communists see it, conflict between the classes is inevitable. They believe the laboring class is bound to win. One day the working class will overthrow the owning class, establish a dictatorship, and dominate the world.

The second important teaching of Communism is that the communist party is the means of speeding up that proletariat victory. To that end they make the communist party a small, well-disciplined, and highly committed group. If you are a communist party member, you are expected to be ready to do anything for the party—work, steal, lie, or give your life if necessary. No sacrifice is too costly or too great. Relatively few Russians are members of the communist party. Two hundred fifty-eight million people are controlled by fewer than 16 million party members—about 6 percent. That is shocking, isn't it?

But party members do not control the communist party. The party controls its members. This is the way it works. At the grass roots, the communist party in every area is organized in small, compact groups. They meet in a home, in a school, or a farm, or in a factory. Each local unit elects a representative to send to the district party council. Party members have no control over the council member they elect. The district council meets and discusses and votes—usually on the recommendations from the council higher up. Once a vote is taken, it becomes binding on every member of the council. Delegates then go back to tell the groups below what the higher council has decided.

Each council sends a representative to a higher body. Each council in turn receives its orders from above. Decisions made by the highest body become binding on every party member. Ultimately, one man becomes the leader-dictator—a Brezhnev or a Castro. In practice, the "people's government" becomes an empty phrase. No other party organization is permitted in a communist country. The communist party holds a tight monopoly on every phase of the nation's life—business, labor, education, army, police. There is no other leadership. There is no other voice.

A third communist doctrine is that religion is a purely man-made institution. Communists are materialists—only the material world is real. In other words, they say man is a material machine. He is shaped by his experience, according to the class in which he was born.

Because they hold this to be true, Communism promises that when its program has been carried out and the class conflict ended, the flaws in human nature will quickly disappear. Man will be a perfect creature. No communist country has ever achieved this goal, but it is the party's dream and promise.

Meanwhile the Communist would argue that there is no good or evil in itself. Lying, sabotage, even murder are good if they help to speed the party goal of worldwide revolution. Anything that hinders the revolution, on the other hand, is evil.

A fourth teaching of the Communists is what they term "dialectical materialism." In simplest terms, it means that they believe in a material universe in which progress comes through crisis. Communists therefore believe that revolution—or more exactly, a series of violent changes, is essential for winning the war against the capitalistic society. That can best be accomplished, they believe, by a succession of advances and retreats.

In the words of Dr. Schwarz, "It is impossible to judge the goal of communism merely by the direction in which they are moving at any given time. The objective is fixed, it does not change. The direction of progress towards the objective reverses itself all the time." A favorite communist technique in a given country is to find some cause—some real or fancied injustice—and rally support in the interests of that cause. In Russia, the communist slogan was Bread, Peace, and Land. Accordingly, in 1917, while coming to power, they distributed land to millions of peasants. In 1928, however, when they had consolidated power, they deprived the peasantry of the land that they themselves had given.

The Deception of Communism

Communism is an evil system, a system to be feared. It is a system rooted deeply in untruth. It promises "people's government," but it gives dictatorship. It denies man's need for God, yet promises to save mankind by revolution. It is deceptive, yet clever and implacable. It changes methods constantly, but it does not change its course.

Today the Communists have conquered more than one and a half billion people on our planet. In addition, they have programs operating in practically every country. Why? To win the world for Communism.

Nikita Khruschev in his day of power said, "Although I am sixty-nine years old and do not have much longer to live, nevertheless I hope to live to see the day that the Red flag covers all the earth."

But you as a Christian ask, What can we do? First, we should stop helping Communism. That does not necessarily mean a breaking off of normal diplomatic relations, but rather a halt to policies that strengthen the communist movement.

Consider the ties sustained by business interests in the United States. Lenin is quoted as predicting that western capitalists "will compete with each other to sell us goods cheaper, and sell them quicker, so that the Soviets will buy from one rather than from the other. . . . They will bring [these goods] themselves," he said, "without thinking about their future."

Aleksandr Solzhenitsyn, the Russian exile and Nobel-Prize-winning author now living in this country, says that is exactly what has happened. The major construction projects in Russia's initial five-year plan were built exclusively with American technology and materials. And now we are beginning to do the same thing in China. Lenin predicted that our greed would result in this.

Another alliance is the one that links our government with theirs. We gave diplomatic recognition to communist Russia in 1933 and entered into a military alliance during World War II, even when Stalin was executing an estimated 40,000 persons every month. Solzhenitsyn reminds us that when the war was over, we gave the Soviet Communists unlimited aid and virtually unlimited concessions. Since then we have let Communists swallow up one country after another around the world. Afghanistan is only the most recent of scores of nations the Communists have taken over.

It is a serious thing to strengthen the hand of one who is intent on doing evil. The Bible warns against alliance with the wicked. The principle of 2 Corinthians 6:14 applies to nations as well as individuals: "Be ye not unequally yoked together with unbelievers."

But there is another potentially more effective thing each of us can do—and this is crucial. We must give ourselves to building a strong and spiritually alive America. Communism expects America to give up eventually, because we have lost the will to resist. They want to bring us to the point where we will no longer sacrifice for freedom. It is a burning, searching question whether the day is approaching when our nation will soon reach the point of believing the slogan Better Red than Dead. As things stand now, it seems we are marching toward defeat. We need to open our eyes, to be valiant for the right, to renew our faith in Jesus Christ and our commitment to His ways of righteousness.

Can America resist? Pray and live and work and witness to the end that our country may turn to God, that we may recover ourselves from self-indulgence and sin and unbelief, that we may stand in the coming day of crisis.

NOTES

1. "Solzhenitsyn on Communism," *Time,* 18 February 1980.
2. Fred Schwarz, "What is Communism?" Published lecture series. Christian Anti-Communism Crusade, Box 890, Long Beach, CA 90809

10

Divine Healing

Is there such a thing as divine healing today? That question is being asked by thousands of people who long for relief from physical sickness. Physical and mental afflictions are common to most of us. Why does God permit His children to suffer? Is illness necessary? Can God heal? Does God heal today? Is it always God's will to heal? What does the Bible teach about healing? Those are some of the questions that I will try to answer.

In the New Testament epistle of James we are reminded that God cares about our afflictions. He is deeply interested in our needs. If any believer is afflicted, says James, "let him pray" (5:13). He also reminds us that when we pray, God "giveth to all men liberally" (James 1:5). Our God is all-loving, all-powerful, all-wise, and He wants the best for His children. God really cares about our needs.

In James 5 we find that this caring God is concerned about our emotional needs. Verse 13 reads, "Is any among you afflicted? Let him pray. Is any merry? Let him sing psalms." The word *afflicted* refers to the difficult experiences of life, and especially the depression and anxiety we encounter because of them. "Is any among you suffering?" James is saying. "Let him pray." What are we to do with the great needs of life? James tells us to bring them to Jesus Christ. Whatever else we do, we are to share our joys and sorrows with the Lord Jesus and talk them over with the loving Father who hears and responds to our afflictions.

Sometimes the problems of life appear to be more than we can handle. In our grief we hardly know where to turn or what to do.

Matthew 14 records such an incident. John the Baptist was brutally murdered. Matthew says of John, "And his head was brought in a charger, and given to the damsel: and she brought it to her mother. And his disciples came, and took up the body, and buried it, and went and told Jesus" (Matthew 14:11-12).

What a traumatic, heartbreaking experience! John's disciples were shattered. What were they to do? They lovingly picked up John's body and carefully buried it and went and told Jesus.

Heartaches of one kind or another come to each of us. And we, too, must turn to Jesus in our hour of grief. It is comforting to realize that He understands our sorrow.

Isaiah described the Lord as "a man of sorrows, and acquainted with grief" (Isaiah 53:3). Jesus as the God-man knew what it was like to be weary. At times He even had no place to lay His head. He knew what it was to be lonely, what it was like to suffer intense pain and even death. Always remember that we have an Intercessor who understands and is touched with our sorrows, our pain, and grief.

But there are not only sad days in life. There are also glad days. Gladness is a wonderful emotion. James asks, "Is any merry? Let him sing psalms" (James 5:13). Happy or sad, cheerful or tearful, James tells us to relate everything to God through prayer and praise. Praise is as much a part of prayer as are petitions. The word *praise* in its various forms is found over five hundred fifty times in the Bible. Paul told the believers at Philippi, "Rejoice in the Lord always: and again I say, Rejoice" (Philippians 4:4). Praise should become habitual.

We find prayer to be an important solution to our emotional needs. But we find in James 5:14-15 that prayer is important to our physical needs as well. "Is any sick among you? let him call for the elders of the church; and let them pray over him, anointing him with oil in the name of the Lord: And the prayer of faith shall save the sick, and the Lord shall raise him up; and if he have committed sins, they shall be forgiven him" (James 5:14-15).

SOME NEGATIVES

Notice what is *not* taught here. *James is not teaching that all sickness is a direct result of sin.* The word "if" in verse 15 suggests that some sickness is not the direct result of sin. As we study the gospels, we find that even Jesus' disciples were confused about the relationship of sin to sickness. In John 9:2-3, the "disciples asked [Jesus], saying, Master, who did sin, this man, or his parents, that he was born blind? Jesus answered, Neither hath this man sinned, nor his parents: but that the works of God should be made manifest in him." The blind man's illness was not a punishment for his or anyone else's sins. It had a greater purpose—that Christ might glorify the Father by healing the man.

At times, sickness *is* a result of sin. Some of the Corinthian Christians were careless concerning the Lord's table, and Paul wrote to tell them, "For this cause many are weak and sickly among you, and many sleep" (1 Corinthians 11:30). In Mark's gospel, Jesus ministered to the man sick of the palsy. First He forgave his sin, and then He healed his body. Jesus forgave his wickedness and then relieved his weakness.

There is no doubt that at times sickness is a direct result of sin, but it is a serious mistake to assume that *all* sickness is because of unconfessed sin. To accuse a sick person of sin is the kind of judgment no human being is capable of making. James 5:14-15 certainly does not teach that all sickness is caused by sin.

Neither is James condemning the use of medicine for healing. Some people believe and teach that we should have nothing whatsoever to do with the medical profession. They assert that consulting doctors or using medicine, hospitals, or other human means reveals a lack of faith in God. But the Bible does not teach that. In fact, many scholars would suggest that the anointing oil of verse 14 was actually used as medicine in Bible times. That seems often to be the case in biblical accounts of illness and treatment. For example, Luke's gospel tells how the good Samaritan applied oil to the wounds of the man he found on the road to Jericho. Also, much of the historical literature of that day confirms that oil was used as a healing medicine.

But whether or not James is referring to the use of medicine, we do find that there are many references to medicine throughout the Bible. In Proverbs 17:22 we read, "A merry heart doeth good like a medicine." Luke was a member of the medical profession. In Colossians 4:14, Paul refers to his co-worker as "Luke, the beloved physician." We find that Paul even prescribed some medicine himself. Writing to timid Timothy, who was suffering from stomach trouble (possibly an ulcer), the apostle suggested that he "drink no longer water, but use a little wine for thy stomach's sake and thine often infirmities" (1 Timothy 5:23).

Actually, Jesus Himself settled the entire controversy. In Matthew 9:12 Jesus said, "They that be whole need not a physician, but they that are sick." Jesus was saying that sick people need a doctor.

So James is neither teaching that all sickness is caused directly by sin, nor condemning the use of medical procedures in seeking healing. What is he teaching?

SOME POSITIVES

First, he is teaching that God is able to heal. There is no doubt as to our faith in that statement. It would be foolish to deny that the all-powerful God who created us can just as easily repair our bodies if that pleases Him. Without any question, God is able to heal the body.

Second, James is teaching that God does heal. Few believers would question God's present activity in the area of healing. The Bible clearly records the exercise of God's power in the healing of the sick. Jesus Himself healed multitudes while He was here on earth and has healed others during the centuries that have elapsed since He ascended to heaven.

Even in my own life, I have experienced God's miraculous healing power. During my junior year at the Moody Bible Institute I was stricken with a malignant tumor. For weeks I was confined to a hospital bed. I experienced two operations and thirty radium treatments. My doctor told me that I might not live and if I did, the hope of having children was only remotely possible.

Right there in my hospital room I prayed, "O Lord, this bed is my altar of consecration. My life is in Your hands. I yield myself to Your will alone. I know You are all-powerful and can do absolutely anything. Thy will be done."

That was more than thirty years ago. God did a healing work in my life that even amazed the doctors. I believe I am living proof that God is able to heal, and He does heal in many instances.

SOME INTERROGATIVES

But, we must ask, *Is it always the will of God to heal?* I realize that there are some brothers and sisters in Christ who answer, emphatically, yes. They contend that it is God's will to heal all sickness—that only sin, or lack of faith, keeps us from being healed. They say that when Jesus Christ atoned for our sins on the cross, He brought about deliverance from all our infirmities.

We agree that Christ's death brought about deliverance. His death did purchase our deliverance from the infirmities of sin. But nowhere in the Scriptures do we find the promise of complete freedom from physical infirmity until Jesus Christ comes again to reign. It is in that day of full redemption that "God shall wipe away all tears from their eyes; and there shall be no more death, neither sorrow, nor crying, neither shall there by any more pain: for the former things are passed away" (Revelation 21:4). In that day we shall know full deliverance from our illnesses.

Some suggest that if we only have enough faith, we can be healed now of all sickness. But that is a difficult position to try to defend from the Scriptures. To argue that the healing of our infirmities depends on our faith would suggest, it seems, that if our faith were great enough, we would never have to die.

Romans 8:22-23 appears to contradict this position. "For we know that the whole creation groaneth and travaileth in pain together until now. And not only they, *but ourselves also,* which have the firstfruits of the Spirit, even we ourselves groan within ourselves, *waiting for the adoption, to wit, the redemption of our body*" (italics added). Paul continues to verse 26, "For we know not what we should pray for as we ought: but the Spirit itself maketh intercession for us." And in verse 27 he writes, "And he that searcheth the hearts knoweth what is the mind of the Spirit, because he maketh intercession for the saints according to the will of God." If the indwelling Holy Spirit prays for our infirmities according to the will of God, who are we to pray any other way?

God may grant healing if, in His wisdom, that is best. But He may allow His children to suffer. Suffering does not necessarily indicate a lack of faith on their part, nor does it indicate a lack of love on God's part. Sometimes we learn more of God's way in sickness than in health, and often we glorify Christ more in suffering than in health.

The apostle Paul was one whom God used greatly in spite of physical affliction. Paul was apparently half-blind. He had to dictate his letters because he was unable to write except in a huge scrawl. To the church at Corinth he wrote, "Lest I should be exalted above measure through the abundance of the revelations, there was given to me a thorn in the flesh, the messenger of Satan to buffet me, lest I should be exalted above measure. For this thing I besought the Lord thrice, that it might depart from me. And he said unto me, My grace is sufficient for thee" (2 Corinthians 12:7-9). Three times Paul prayed for physical deliverance. God's answer was, "My grace is sufficient." Paul understood that it is not always God's will to heal.

We might also ask, "What does James mean by 'the prayer of faith'?" Personally, I do not believe that the prayer of faith refers to ordinary prayer, no matter how good and earnest it may be. On one occasion Paul had to leave his sick friend Trophimus behind. Paul was a man of great faith, and surely he must have earnestly prayed for his afflicted friend. Apparently, the "prayer of faith" cannot be prayed simply at will. It is my conviction that the faith necessary to pray the kind of prayer James is speaking of is given of God in certain cases to serve His purposes and to accomplish

His sovereign will.

Can God heal our afflictions? Yes, He is able, and He often works powerfully in the lives of some of His children. But is there healing for us all? No, not until the day we receive our glorious resurrected bodies. Until that day, we must daily submit ourselves to the will of God—nothing more, nothing less, and nothing else.

> My Jesus, as Thou wilt! O may Thy will be mine;
> Into Thy hand of love I would my all resign.
> Thro' sorrow or thro' joy, Conduct me as Thine own;
> And help me still to say, My Lord, Thy will be done.
>
> My Jesus, as Thou wilt! All shall be well for me,
> Each changing future scene I gladly trust with Thee.
> Straight to my home above I travel calmly on,
> And sing, in life or death, "My Lord, Thy will be done."
>
> Benjamin Schmolck

11

How to Keep the Faith

Christian institutions, like people, are born to live and serve. But, like individuals, they are susceptible to death. The mortality rate of Christian schools is especially evident when we look at the early history of our country. Some of America's oldest and most prestigious colleges and universities began as virile Christian institutions. But the light of Christian testimony flickered and went out.

Harvard College was founded in 1638 with a special view of training pastors. Until 1700 more than half its graduates went into the ministry. The early Harvard handbook set out the knowledge of God and Jesus Christ as the principal end of life. But by 1869, spiritual Harvard lay on its deathbed, as the university was presided over by an enemy of the Christian faith.

Yale, from its beginning in 1701, was more conservative. In 1795 its president addressed students on such subjects as "The Bible Is the Word of God." In 1825 a Yale gospel group traveled about the country in evangelistic ministry. But Yale's once evangelical stance has long since disappeared. Fifty-four percent of a recent graduating class said they had no belief in any God.

Dartmouth College was founded to train men as missionaries to the American Indians. Princeton in its early days insisted that the faculty be "convinced of the necessity of religious experience for salvation." Yet both soon left their orthodox paths and secularized. Many other well-known schools had similar beginnings—and similar fates.

As once-Christian schools became secularized, churches and individuals stepped into the breach. They established new Christian schools and training institutions. Of these, the greater number have drifted from their original moorings. The mortality rate is high, even today.

How can a Bible-believing school maintain a faithful stand in these turbulent times? The question is important to every church and every Christian, for tomorrow's leaders—pastors and Christian workers, as well as laymen—are being shaped by the Christian schools of today. No Christian school falls by itself. It brings down other organizations with it. With no exception I know of, every professing Christian group floundering in the quicksand of unbelief today can trace its trouble to the failure of its schools.

How can our Christian schools be conserved for the Christian ministry? There is no easy answer. But let me suggest some possible guidelines that may help us fight "the good fight of faith" (1 Timothy 6:12).

KNOW THE FAITH

First, if we are to keep the faith, we must know the faith. It must be virile and well-defined. We cannot safeguard a nebulous, shibbolethlike shadow, hidden in a closet.

The great evangelist George Whitefield once asked a coal miner in Cornwall, England, what he believed.

"Oh," the miner replied, "I believe what my church believes."

"And what does your church believe?" the evangelist inquired.

"Well, the church believes what I believe."

"But what do you both believe?" Whitefield persisted.

Still the miner would not be cornered. "We both believe the same thing," he retorted.

An elusive faith can never be defended. The Word of God tells us that we are to "be ready always to give an answer to every man that asketh [us] a reason of the hope that is in [us] with meekness and fear" (1 Peter 3:15).

The foundation of our faith is the Word of God. Speaking

seventy-five years ago, Dr. Benjamin Warfield warned: "The Word of the living God is our sole assurance that there has been a redemptive activity exercised by God in the world. Just in proportion as our confidence in this Word shall wane, in just that proportion shall we lose our hold upon the fact of a redemptive work of God in the world."

Our faith rests in the inspired Word of God. The Moody Bible Institute's doctrinal statement reads, "The Bible, including both the Old and the New Testaments, is a divine revelation, the original autographs of which were verbally inspired by the Holy Spirit."

God's Word makes the same claim for itself. "All scripture is given by inspiration of God, and is profitable for doctrine, for reproof, for correction, for instruction in righteousness: That the man of God may be perfect, throughly furnished unto all good works" (2 Timothy 3:16-17). The expression "given by inspiration of God" means "God-breathed." God is the source of the Scripture; it comes from Him, just as if it were His breath, in such a way that it is His own expression word for word. "For the prophecy came not in old time by the will of man; but holy men of God spake as they were moved by the Holy Ghost" (2 Peter 1:21). If *all* Scripture is inspired, no Scripture is uninspired. *Verbal inspiration* means that the very *words* of Scripture are God-breathed. Our faith rests upon the *inerrant* Word of God. To quote Dr. Alfred Martin, "Because some people have tried to restrict the infallibility of the Bible only to the area of faith and morals, it is also helpful to use the word *inerrant* in describing it. When we say that the Bible is inerrant, we mean that there are no errors of any kind whatever in it. 'That is *infallible* which makes, or is capable of making, no mistakes; that is *inerrant* which contains no errors' [*Webster's Collegiate Dictionary*]. The Bible is both infallible and inerrant."

William Lyon Phelps of Yale, sometimes called the most beloved professor in America, said, "I thoroughly believe in university education for both men and women, but I believe a knowledge of the Bible without a college course is more valuable than a college course without the Bible." If Christian schools are to keep the faith, we must have the same attitude—an attitude of total trust in the Word of God.

AFFIRM THE FAITH

It is not enough, however, to know the faith. We must consistently affirm the faith. Biblical Christianity is contrary to the natural man, and it cannot be maintained without constant struggle. We must fight the good fight of faith.

Not only must the faith be affirmed before opponents, but it must be reaffirmed among ourselves as well. Deuteronomy 6 sets a pattern for the family that must be followed by all believers. Notice the fourfold command from Scripture: "And these words, which I command thee this day, shall be in thine heart: And thou shalt *teach them* diligently unto thy children, and shalt *talk of them* when thou sittest in thine house, and when thou walkest by the way, and when thou liest down, and when thou risest up. And thou shalt *bind them* for a sign upon thine hand, and they shall be as frontlets between thine eyes. And thou shalt *write them* upon the posts of thy house, and on thy gates" (Deuteronomy 6:6-9, italics added).

God's people were to know the faith, to teach the faith, to talk the faith, to live the faith, and to write the faith for all to see. But even after all that, they were warned, "Beware lest thou forget the Lord" (v. 12).

How can a Christian institution affirm the faith? First, by making known its doctrinal stand so that no one can miss it. We at the Moody Bible Institute do this annually in our catalog and, as much as possible, in other public statements. We feel a deep responsibility to make known the essence not only of what we are but also of what we believe and teach.

Second, a school can affirm its faith by stressing it among faculty, administration, and students. Once a year every person in a key position at Moody Bible Institute—teachers, administrators, even our trustees—re-reads our doctrinal statement thoughtfully and seriously, signing it to show his recommitment. Members of our faculty and staff are chosen in the light of their attitudes toward our doctrinal position as much as on the basis of their educational qualifications. Prospective faculty members are carefully interviewed by our director of personnel, our dean of education, and the president. We review their eschatology (theology of end times), their attitude toward Christian separation, and their commitment to personal soul winning. Preventive medicine is far less costly than emergency treatment later.

Often schools have drifted because, in seeking to improve academically, they have sacrificed the heart of their original commitment to Jesus Christ and a needy world. Our goal is academic excellence coupled with personal faith, commitment to and love for Christ.

We expect our faculty and staff to reaffirm the faith in their personal lives and work as well as in the classroom. As president, I attempt to do that in our weekly chapel sessions, in which we touch on the basic themes of Christian life and ministry. I also recall the events that led to the founding of our school.

Once every year I speak on how to lead a soul to Christ, how to know the will of God, and the importance of a daily quiet time. I also speak on our view of the church and on our position as servants of the church. We see these truths as basic. In repeating them we reaffirm our faith.

Why do schools drift? Because of individuals. And individuals drift because they lack a stated purpose. The person who has no target is not likely to shoot many arrows. The uncommitted mind is the drifting mind.

A school must not only make known its doctrinal position; it must enforce it as well. Harvard College, now Harvard University, for example, permitted freedom in matters of theology. It also failed to set any kind of standards of spiritual commitment for its officers. True, such measures will not always prevent drifting. Andover Theological Seminary attempted to require conformance to the Westminster Confession, only to have this requirement set aside by court ruling. Princeton, on the other hand, seems to have been overpowered as a result of granting degrees to non-Christians. Eventually pressure from secular-minded alumni forced the school to desert its evangelical thrust.

We do not apologize for our doctrinal statement or try to hide it. We publicize it. When asked, "Where does Moody stand?" I am happy to say, "Moody Bible Institute stands where we have stood since our inception. We have not altered our theological stance in any way, nor do we intend to do so." By the grace of God, we want to walk humbly, yet courageously, in the steps of those men who have gone before—men like Moody, Torrey, Gray, Houghton, and Culbertson.

Our message is the tried and proved gospel of Jesus Christ. Our passion is to see lost people converted and added to the family of God. Our motive is the constraining love of Christ. Our attitude is that of faith in a living Savior who delights to do abundantly above what we ask or think. Our method is serving people. In all these things we unashamedly affirm the faith.

Undergird the Faith

But more than doctrine is involved. *A Christian school must also undergird the faith.* The New Testament word for "church" is *ekklesia,* which means "called out ones." A truly Christian institution, by its very nature, is called out to a superior life-style. We believe that a position of separation is essential to keeping the faith. Students may complain occasionally about rules and regulations, but if nothing else, they are a reminder that the Christian's life-style is different.

Conformity to the world would merely show that we were drifting. We are mindful of the emphasis of Romans 12:2 brought out with special clarity in the Phillips translation: "Don't let the world around you squeeze you into its own mold." We reject the pressure to conform to this world.

We also undergird our faith by a positive program of training. Christian separation is separation *from* the world and *unto* Jesus Christ. Such separation demands cultivation of the inner life. We strive to encourage the devotional life through a daily quiet time. Throughout the year we try to make ours a climate conducive to spiritual growth.

SHARE THE FAITH

Finally, we must share the faith. An organization that does not share the faith will ultimately not keep the faith. A Christian organization must share the faith for the same reasons that constrain the individual Christian to do so.

We must share the faith, first of all, because of our knowledge. Paul declares in Romans 1:14, "I am [a] debtor." We owe the world a debt because of what we know.

Some years ago Dr. Jonas Salk discovered the final phases of the polio vaccine. He had a means of freeing the world from the suffering and pain caused by the dreaded disease polio. Suppose he had decided to withhold that lifesaving vaccine. Such action would have been criminal.

In the same way, Christians have the truth that can free people from the power of sin. Can we sit idly by and watch people die in sin without giving them the good news that Christ died for them? Of course we cannot—if we really accept the truths of God's Word. We must share the faith because of our knowledge.

Second, we must share the faith because of our blessings. Like the lepers of 2 Kings 7:9, we should remind ourselves, "We do not well: this is a day of good tidings, and we hold our peace." Contrary to the view of many people today, the world does not owe us a thing. But believers owe the world an intelligent, loving presentation of God's good news.

The Old Testament prophet Ezekiel presents an answer to the question "Why share the faith?" Listen to the Lord's words to him.

> When I say unto the wicked, O wicked man, thou shalt surely die; if thou dost not speak to warn the wicked from his way, that wicked man shall die in his iniquity; but his blood will I require at thine hand. Nevertheless, if thou warn the wicked of his way to

turn from it; if he do not turn from his way, he shall die in his iniquity; but thou hast delivered thy soul. [Ezekiel 33:8-9]

God is telling Ezekiel that he has the privilege and responsibility to warn people. Failure to sound the warning would result in his being held accountable. The same principle applies to Christians today. We must share because of our blessings.

Third, we must share the faith because of the Great Commission. "Go ye into all the world" (Mark 16:15) applies to us. William Carey read Matthew 28 and was burdened for a perishing, unbelieving world. He thought, "Does this commission of Jesus apply to me? Does God really want me to go as a missionary to share the good news?" Carey decided to share his burden for witnessing with the local ministerium. The presiding pastor sternly rebuked young Carey and informed him that when God wanted to save the heathen, He would do it without his help. In spite of that rebuke, William Carey responded to the commission given by Jesus. He accepted his responsibility to share the good news and became a missionary to India.

Just as God the Father sent His Son into this world, so God the Son sends each of us to communicate His love. This divine succession brings to us an awesome responsibility. "As my Father hath sent me, " said Jesus, "even so send I you" (John 20:21). We must share the faith because of the Great Commission.

Finally, we must share the faith because of our position. "We are ambassadors for Christ . . . we pray you in Christ's stead, be ye reconciled to God" (2 Corinthians 5:20). It is sobering to realize that God is making His appeal to the lost world through you and me. Charles B. Williams translates 2 Corinthians 5:20 powerfully: "So I am an envoy to represent Christ, because it is through me that God is making His appeal. As one representing Christ, I beg you, be ye reconciled to God."

With that awesome position, we are very much responsible. Each Christian is either a good ambassador of Christ or a poor one, but we cannot escape the fact that we are ambassadors. In the light of that staggering truth, accept your position with great care. We must share the faith because of our position.

The great preacher Alexander Maclaren pointed out that "Christianity is the only religion that has ever passed through periods of decadence and purified itself again. Men have gone back to the Word and laid hold again of it in its simple omnipotence, and so a decadent Christianity has sprung up again into purity and power."

I believe that is true. But what tragic loss there has been where those entrusted with keeping the faith have failed, especially in Christian schools. Again and again, such collapses have been responsible for tragic attacks against the church, attacks made from within.

We have a charge to keep, and with God's help we must be faithful. Each generation must in turn fight the good fight of truth and keep the faith. The only way is loyalty to the Word of God and to Jesus Christ, the living Word. By God's grace and with His help, no generation need fail nor falter. In our day **we** must keep the faith.

12

A Call for National Renewal

Some historians have told us that we are living in the closing hours of a dying culture. Many of our world's great cities are threatened by corruption and violence. The dark clouds of war hover dangerously over the Middle East. Red China, now a major power, appears anxious to display its muscles. Russia has flagrantly committed open aggression and seems to be daring the world to react. In many places, common sense and reason have been replaced by mob rule.

Morality in the United States is virtually nonexistent. Crime is on the increase. Most of our universities have become centers of humanism and secularism. Poverty and illiteracy predominate in many areas.

The late J. Edgar Hoover said, "We face the twin enemies of crime and Communism. Crime and moral decay are eating at us from within. And Communism stands ready to pick up the pieces."

Amid all this, a large segment of the church of Jesus Christ has adopted the spirit of this age and is apostate. Situation ethics and the "new morality" have been encouraged, and the masses are blinded to God's truth, God's will, and God's redemption. We desperately need a national call to repentance. It is no secret that we need help. But few realize that our hope as a nation lies in the hands of God's people.

When Seneca, the Roman philosopher and teacher, warned his day of the weakness of the Roman Empire, people laughed at him. To Roman citizens living in the glitter of success, inspired by their magnificent buildings, tree-lined avenues, gushing fountains, and triumphant arches, Rome was unbeatable. Rome was the eternal city.

It seemed absurd to think that war, taxation, crime, race riots, subversion, and apathy would prevail. But Rome fell—the impossible happened.

And now, the causes for the fall of Rome are increasingly prominent in our society! Divorce is bulldozing the family to ruin; for every three marriages in the United States, there is one divorce. Taxes are climbing steadily, and inflation continues to eat away at our standard of living. Pleasure is an obsession to the majority of people. In 1970 a total of 80 billion dollars was spent for national defense. Religion is in a state of compromise and sleep. The five fundamental reasons for the fall of Rome are now glaringly evident in our nation.

Several years ago Roger Babson, newspaper journalist, stated in an article that the measure of the strength of a nation is the intellectual and spiritual growth of its people, not its monetary gains. In fact, material prosperity often leads to the ruin of a nation. The only movement that will save a nation is a spiritual revival, because people are then more interested in serving, in seeking strength rather than security, and in pursuing character more than profit.

That is very upsetting, isn't it? But if we honestly face ourselves and our national condition, there is hope. We need divine help! We need national repentance. We need a spiritual revival.

WHAT REVIVAL IS NOT

Unfortunately many people seem to have a false idea of what revival is. Revival is not large crowds. All of us have witnessed large religious gatherings where thousands attended, but by no stretching of the definition could that be called revival. Revival is not great preaching. As a boy, I listened to the great George Truett. I had never heard such preaching, but that was not revival. Revival is not even people's being converted. Where genuine revival exists, people usually are converted. But in the true sense of the word, revival is not the salvation of the lost.

What Is Revival?

Then what does the word *revival* mean? The word *revival* comes from two Latin words: *re*, which means "again," and *vivo*, which means "to live." The literal meaning is "to live again." Charles Finney, the great evangelist, defined revival as "a new beginning of obedience to God . . . just as in the case of a converted sinner, the first step in a deep repentance, a breaking down of heart, a getting down in the dust before God, with deep humility and a forsaking of sin." J. Edwin Orr simply calls revival "times of refreshing from the Lord."

Revival in the spiritual realm is to love Jesus Christ in a new and significant way. To be revived is to regain spiritual consciousness.

God's Prescription for Revival

About once a year I come down with a severe head and chest cold. Immediately I phone my doctor. He, in turn, gives me a good prescription. If I act and do what the prescription requires, I am fine within a few days.

The Bible contains a divine prescription for revival. It is God's medicine for moral and spiritual sickness, and it is found in 2 Chronicles 7:14. "If my people, who are called by my name, shall humble themselves, and pray, and seek my face, and turn from their wicked ways; then will I hear from heaven, and will forgive their sin, and will heal their land." God promises to do His part in revival, but it is conditional. Let us review together the ingredients of God's prescription.

Look first at the words *"If my people, who are called by my name."* Do you know where revival begins? Revival begins with the people of God. Have you received Jesus Christ as your Savior? If so, you are God's child. God is your Father, and you are part of God's wonderful family. Revival begins in the lives of those of us who are in God's family.

Some time ago I concluded a study in the book of Jonah. Let me share with you what I discovered. When Jonah repented of his rebellion, his indifference, and his prejudice, God caused the people of Nineveh to repent. The greatest obstacle to the conversion of Nineveh was not to be found in Nineveh. It was not the sin and corruption of the Ninevites, although those were great. It was not the graft-ridden police force of corrupt politicians. It was not the false cults and religions. The biggest obstacle to the salvation of Nineveh was found in the heart of a pious, prejudiced man named Jonah. There was no deceitfulness in all of Nineveh like the deceitfulness in Jonah's heart.

Jonah was the key to the salvation of Nineveh. And God's people are the keys to the spiritual climate of our nation and the world. That means that you and I have a big responsibility. Revival starts with us, and if it is to come to our nation, it must come through us. God's prescription for revival begins with a humbling of the individual.

The second step to revival is found in the words, *"If my people . . . shall humble themselves."* Take a look at this word *humble*. It means "not proud," or "not arrogant, but modest, broken." The message of James 4:6 is powerful: "Wherefore he saith, God resisteth the proud, but giveth grace unto the humble."

Have you ever had to work with someone who really made life difficult for you? He resisted every idea you had and everything you said. He fought you at every turn. Things were not comfortable, were they? Can you imagine anything as helpless and hopeless as having Almighty God resist you? Are we proud people? Brokenness and humility are key steps in meeting God's prescription for revival. Paul prayed with tears day and night. David Brainerd, suffering a slow, painful death from tuberculosis, interceded for the souls of the American Indians. Dr. William Culbertson, former president and chancellor at Moody Bible Institute, would often say to us in chapel, "Walk humbly before God." His life was an example of his words.

Approximately 3 billion people on our earth need to see the power of God displayed! God tells us that we are the key to our nation's spiritual condition. Revival begins with God's people, with individuals. The theme of our day is the mass man. We live in a day of computers and collectivism. But here we see that God deals with the individual. "Revive *me*, O Lord," is our plea.

Self-examination on the part of the Lord's people is imperative. As long as Christians are unbroken, unconcerned, unimpressed, and unforgiving, revival cannot come. We must say with Elihu, "If I have done iniquity, I will do no more" (Job 34:32).

There is a third ingredient in God's prescription, and that is prayer. Second Chronicles 7:14 says, *"If my people . . . shall . . . pray."* You ask, For what shall we pray? Through the prophet Hosea, God said, "Break up your fallow ground: for it is time to seek the LORD (Hosea 10:12). Fallow ground is dry ground, unproductive ground. We need to pray that we might become productive Christians, instruments fit for the Master's use.

Job was a good man, yet he was not released from his captivity until he prayed for his miserable comforters. Prayer has a boomerang effect; it blesses the one who does the praying.

We need to pray for revival in our hearts, in our schools, in our churches, and in this nation. Our prayers should be definite. We need to pray for complete yieldedness to the Holy Spirit. God through Zechariah said, "Not by might, nor by power, but by my spirit" (Zechariah 4:6). Complete dependence upon the Spirit's leadership is the only method.

Revival has always found power through prayer. Go back with me through the centuries to A.D. 30. The city is Jerusalem. The evangelist is a bold, untutored fisherman named Peter. The occasion is a Jewish holiday when Jews and God-fearing Gentiles have gathered from all over the known world. Peter powerfully proclaims Jesus Christ. Three thousand people receive Christ that very day. The secret of the harvest was the power of the Holy Spirit activated by the prayers of God's people.

Move on. The year is 1872. The city is London, and the evangelist is a relatively unknown YMCA worker from America, D. L. Moody. On a Sunday evening, Moody is preaching in a North London church. He asks those who have decided for Christ to stand. During the past few days, over four hundred people have made decisions for Christ. Ultimately thousands came to Christ through the ministry of Moody. What was the cause? God's people were praying.

God wants to start with you and me. Do you want Him to revive you? Can you pray, "Here I am, Lord. You're the Potter; I'm merely the clay. Begin Your revival in me right now. Change me. Make me usable, and let me aid in bringing revival to our world."

God's formula continues: *"If my people . . . shall . . . seek my face."* To seek God's face is not a quick "Lord bless me, my wife, and our two children." It demands determination, steadfastness, singleness of heart, and perseverance. John Welch, the Scottish preacher, felt that a day was misspent if he did not spend eight to ten hours in prayer for the needs of his congregation. Once when the English writer John Ruskin was trying to complete a book and did not want to be distracted, he published a notice: "John Ruskin is totally engaged in completing a book and therefore unable to answer calls or correspondence. Consider him dead for the next three months."

We need to seek God's face with that kind of determination and perseverance!

God gives the final step: *"If my people . . . shall . . . turn from their wicked ways."* When ancient Israel finally dealt with the sin of Achan, there was victory. For them to turn from what was wrong meant repentance. As long as David continued in sin, he lacked fellowship, power, and the blessing of God. He was a liability rather than a asset. Then, he faced his sin, confessed it, and repented fully. Restoration began only after repentance. When the early church dealt with Ananias and Sapphira (Acts 5), it started to move ahead again. The same thing will happen in our lives when we deal with our sin.

Repentance is often difficult because many times we are not sensitive to our sin. Sin is smothered and camouflaged in our day. Sin has been driven underground. These days few people experience true conviction. Instead of repenting and confessing sin, they visit a psychiatrist who shows them how to lay the blame for their guilt on an austere father or an overprotective mother, or tells them that they act the way they do because they were underprivileged or overdisciplined in childhood.

But sin has never changed, and we have to learn to face it openly and honestly. God hates sin! God's message to us is *Repent.* In fact, the last word of Jesus Christ to the church was not, as many think, the Great Commission. The Great Commission is the program for the church, but the message of Christ to the churches of Revelation 2 and 3, in reality Christ's final message to the church, was "repent."

Now, let me be exceedingly practical. What can we as individual citizens and Christians do? How can we obey God's command to turn from our wicked ways? First, we can develop the desire to know Jesus Christ better. We should have a holy dissatisfaction. The contented Christian is the sterile Christian. Paul said in effect, "Jesus arrested me on the Damascus road. Now I want to lay hold of all that for which I was arrested by God." We too ought to be thoroughly dissatisfied with our spiritual posture.

Second, we should pray for a change in our lives. I think of Jacob's wrestling with God. He wanted blessing. He would not be denied. Throw your entire life into the will of God. Seek God's very best.

Third, we must commit ourselves to obedience. If we pray for revival and neglect witnessing, we are guilty of hypocrisy. To pray for growth and neglect the local church is absolute foolishness. To pray that we will mature, and then neglect the Word of God is incongruous. We must put ourselves in the way of blessing through obedience.

Fourth, our repentance must be complete. "Create in me a clean heart," David sobbed in Psalm 51:10. For a whole year David had been out of fellowship with God. But he confessed his sin; he turned from his sin; then he could sing again; he could write again; he could pray again. His repentance was total and without reservation.

Fifth, we need to make the crooked straight. If we owe debts, we must pay them, or at least have an understanding with the people we owe. Zacchaeus said, "Lord, the half of my goods I give to the poor; and if I have taken any thing from any man by false accusation, I restore him fourfold" (Luke 19:8). As much as possible, he made the crooked straight.

Sixth, we should develop a seriousness of purpose. It is not easy to keep off the detours, but we should let nothing deflect the magnetic needle of our calling. If there is anything that is a Trojan horse in our day, it is the television set. We must beware lest it rob us of our passion and purpose.

Finally, we have to major in majors. The Christian life requires specialists. We need to have a singleness of heart and purpose. Jesus said in effect, "Be a one-eyed man" (cf. Luke 11:34-36). Paul said, "This one thing I do" (Philippians 3:13). Too many of us burn up too much energy without engaging in things that bring us nearer to God. We must refuse to rust out. Let us start sharing our faith; let us make ourselves available. Let us back our decision with our time and talent and dollars. And let us ask God for great faith in Him. We must begin to expect great things.

Notice what God promises to do if we obey according to 2 Chronicles 7:14: "Then will I hear from heaven, and will forgive their sin, and will heal their land." If God's people will meet the conditions, then God promises to hear, forgive, and heal our land. If we do our part, God will do His part. May we humbly seek God's forgiveness and then give ourselves to be a channel of blessing to our beloved nation.

The Greek word for man is *anthropos,* "the up-looking one." We are to look up, but we are also to hook up. James 1:6 says that we are to ask "in faith, nothing wavering. For he that wavereth is like a wave of the sea driven . . . and tossed." God is saying, "Come alive!" He is saying, "Look up; hook up!" May we realize there is human responsibility and human opportunity. Let us stir up the gift that God has planted in us and seek the outpouring from heaven that our nation so greatly needs!

R. A. Torrey, the second president of the Moody Bible

Institute, often shared God's formula for national recovery: Revival in a church or community is brought about by Christians getting right with God, then praying for revival till God answers that prayer, and finally making themselves available to be used in God's service in winning others to Christ.

Today we call upon each Christian in our beloved nation to meet these conditions. Are *you* willing to pay the price?

13

What Makes a Nation Great?

"It was the best of times: it was the worst of times . . ."

Charles Dickens used those thought-provoking words to open his famous novel *A Tale of Two Cities*. Although they described Europe in the early eighteenth century, they could properly be used to picture our United States today.

We live in the best of times and the worst of times. Scientifically, we have seen fantastic advances. Man has attained such speed in travel that he now looks forward to exploring the solar system. He has split and fused the atom, which has given him the key to enormous unleashed power. The field of communications has literally exploded. First there was the human voice, then writing, then the breakthrough of the printing press, then radio, and now, worldwide television—even live television from the moon. Our world today is indeed a global village.

The technical advance has reached much farther than we realize. Some time ago I was in the jungles of the Yucatan Peninsula to study the ruins of the ancient Mayan civilization. In the middle of nowhere I came upon a one-room, thatched-roof hut with a television antenna proudly pointing toward the sky. "Do you see what I see?" I asked my associates. We entered the very simple one-room house and found a modern television set!

Yes, in many ways these are the best of times. But in other ways they are the worst of times. Technology has brought a host of benefits, but it has also brought its difficulties.

Take one of our more simple problems, for example. We live in rectangular boxes we call houses. They keep heat in and hold cold out. But inside the boxes it is too warm for food; so we build another rectangular box to keep food cold inside the box we made to keep us warm. But inside the box for food it gets too cold for butter; so we make another box to keep the butter warm.

Although advancing civilization has provided solutions for many problems, it has created many others. Along with heart transplants, computers, and supersonic travel, it has also given us nuclear warfare, the problems of the pill, and the tragedy of abortion.

A traveler today can circle the globe in a matter of hours, but millions of people are confused about the directions of their daily lives. Illegal drugs infest our youth cultures from junior high school through college. Crime is rampant in our streets. Corruption spreads like creeping mold from Washington to Watsonville.

One of our great historians, Arnold Toynbee, writes of nineteen major civilizations that have existed since man began to structure government. Of the nineteen, no more than five remain. Our Western civilization is among them. Today we are asking with growing concern, "Will it survive?"

A former secretary of the Department of Health, Education and Welfare, John W. Gardner, has written some probing books concerning the life and death of civilizations. In one of them, *No Easy Victories,* he writes powerfully:

> Back of every great civilization, behind all the power and wealth, is something as powerful . . . a set of ideas, attitudes, convictions and the confidence that those ideas and convictions are viable.
>
> No nation can achieve greatness unless it believes in something—and unless that something has the moral dimensions to sustain a great civilization.[1]

Then Gardner goes on to cite this illustration:

> In Guatemala and southern Mexico one can observe the Indians who were without doubt the lineal descendants of those who created the Mayan civilization. Today they are a humble people,

not asking much of themselves or the world, and not getting much. A light went out![2]

A light went out! What light? And what made it go out? What is the light that sets apart our Western civilization? Do we really know? If we do not, how do we know that it, too, will not flicker and go out?

Alexis de Tocqueville, the famous French political philosopher, visited America when this nation was very young, to find the secret of our greatness. He traveled from town to town, talking with people and asking questions. He examined our young national government, our schools, and our centers of business, without finding the reason for our strength.

Not till he visited the churches of America and witnessed the pulpits of this land "aflame with righteousness" did he find the secret of our greatness. Returning to France, he summarized his findings with this word of warning: "America is great because America is good, and if America ever ceases to be good, America will cease to be great."

Was de Tocqueville right? If America's strength lies in her goodness, our light is going out. It is time we ask ourselves what is true greatness, what has been our light, and what has made it burn with brightness?

Contrary to the thinking of many, greatness is not measured in muscles or missiles. It is not calculated in silver or gold. It is not found in the things that we can see and handle. And because true greatness is measured in unseen qualities, it appears unspectacular and it is tragically neglected.

Greatness is a quality of the inner person. Greatness is found in what we are rather than in what we have. Greatness is a quality of the heart and mind and soul! The Bible gives much insight here. If I were to ask you to name the greatest person pictured by the Word of God, excluding Jesus Christ, whom would you name?

Perhaps you would think of Moses the lawgiver, or Joshua the deliverer of Israel. Or you might choose Mary the mother of Jesus, or Paul the greatest missionary of all time.

But what of John the Baptist?

Jesus identified John as the greatest person who had ever lived until that time. "Among those that are born of women," He said, "there is not a greater prophet than John the Baptist" (Luke 7:28). John's greatness, in fact, had been foretold. Before his birth an angel had said of him, "He shall be great in the sight of the Lord" (Luke 1:15).

Look closely at the life of John the Baptist and you will find specific qualities of greatness. Those same qualities must characterize our lives if our nation is to continue to be great. What are those qualities?

HUMILITY

First, John reflected a spirit of humanity and service. One day a very important committee from Jerusalem came to visit John. Because of his eloquence and popularity, they asked, "Are you the Messiah?"

John answered honestly, "I am not. . . . I am the voice of one crying in the wilderness, Make straight the way of the Lord" (John 1:21-23). He was saying, "I am not the way; I am only the one who shows the way." John walked modestly.

The very next day something exciting happened to John. Jesus came to the Jordan to be baptized. John was amazed. "Baptize you?" he said. "I have need to be baptized by You, and do You come to me?" (Matthew 3:14, NASB). Before that John had said, "One mightier than I cometh, the latchet of whose shoes I am not worthy to unloose" (Luke 3:16). Later, he said of Jesus, "He must increase, but I must decrease" (John 3:30). Powerful John the Baptist served in humility.

Not long ago a national news magazine devoted forty-four pages to the subject of leadership. Many educators and statesmen were quoted concerning their insights as to the essence of leadership. Some defined it as charisma, talent, or know-how, but no one suggested the definition given in the Bible: that of humble service.

Jesus said in Matthew 18:4, "Whosoever therefore shall humble himself as this little child, the same is greatest in the kingdom of heaven." He also declared this principle after His disciples began to argue about rank in their group. "Whosoever will be great among you," He told them, "let him be your minister" (Matthew 20:26). Concern for the good of others is a virtue that made America great. The capacity to care for others and to serve is what gives life significance.

Jesus Christ not only taught humility and service, He also lived it. "For even the Son of man came not to be ministered unto," He said, "but to minister, and to give his life a ransom for many" (Mark 10:45).

In John 13:4-5 we read that Jesus rose from supper "and laid aside his garments; and took a towel . . . and began to wash the disciples' feet." The son of God in humility served men. The symbol of greatness is not necessarily an eagle or a sword or a dollar sign; a more appropriate symbol would be a towel.

In the book *The Ugly American* an Asian journalist writes, "Poor America. It took the British a hundred years to lose their prestige in Asia. American has managed to lose hers in ten years."[3] The book in general gives the impression that we are loud, ostentatious, self-centered, and, worst of all, proud and haughty.

George Washington, kneeling in prayer at Valley Forge, tells us something about the heartbeat of the founders of America. We need to remember that the method of all leadership is humble, modest service. What else makes a nation great?

HONESTY

Second, John possessed integrity and courage. Proverbs 11:3 sets out the importance of this quality: "The integrity of the upright shall guide them: but the perverseness of transgressors shall destroy them." Simply put, honesty builds but dishonesty destroys.

For many years Dr. Madison Sarratt taught mathematics at Vanderbilt University. Before giving exams he would say, "Today I am giving two examinations—one in trigonometry and the other in honesty. I hope you will pass them both. If you must fail one, fail trigonometry. There are many good people in the world who can't pass trigonometry, but there are no good people who cannot pass the examination of honesty." Honesty is the name of the game. Yet many in our land are sick with the disease of dishonesty.

John the Baptist possessed integrity and courage. Jesus said of him in Matthew 11:8, "What went ye out for to see? A man clothed in soft raiment? Behold, they that wear soft clothing are in king's houses." No, John was not a weak, flimsy reed, but a rock. He was not a soft, permissive, wishy-washy, spineless wonder, but an honest man. To those who were false and dishonest John the Baptist said, "O generation of vipers, who hath warned you to flee from the wrath to come?" (Matthew 3:7).

I am afraid that ours is the day of the placid pulpit and the comfortable pew. Dante said, "The hottest place in hell is reserved for those who, in time of crisis, preserved their neutrality." May God grant us integrity and courage.

Noah Webster defines honesty as "honorable; characterized by integrity and straightforwardness in conduct, in thought, and in speech." Integrity means "soundness of moral principle and character."

But our country is not known for its soundness of moral character. White-collar crime costs this nation $40 billion every year. Our nation's hotels and motels spend $500 million per year just to replace items carried off by guests, and one first-class New York City hotel replaces 2,000 towels each month. Shoplifters in Illinois get away with some $800 million worth of merchandise each year. The FBI says that this kind of stealing has increased 221 percent since 1960. Exodus 20:15 needs to be heard across America: "Thou shalt not steal."

In 1973, for the first time in the thirty-six year history of the All-American Soap Box Derby competition, a winner was disqualified for cheating. He forfeited his first-place trophy and a $7,500 college scholarship when X-rays disclosed that an electromagnet and battery had been rigged in the nose of his vehicle, giving him extra starting impetus. Said the county prosecuter: "It's like seeing apple pie, motherhood, and the

American flag grinding to a halt!" Without doubt we are witnessing an erosion of integrity!

John the Baptist was straight. John told his generation, "Bring forth fruits for repentance" (Matthew 3:8). John said, "Every tree which bringeth not forth good fruit is hewn down, and cast into the fire" (Matthew 3:10). John called for repentance and righteousness. One day John stood before the most powerful person in the nation, King Herod. This man had seduced his brother's wife, Herodias, and was living in open immorality. Courageously John said, "It is not lawful for you to have your brother's wife" (Mark 6:18, NASB). That is the type of courage and truth we need today.

When John Huss was about to be burned to death, they asked him to give up his teachings. Huss answered, "What I have taught with my lips, I now seal with my blood." That is courage!

The signing of the Declaration of Independence took courage. When Charles Carroll signed his name, some asked, "How will anyone know which Charles Carroll is meant among all those with that name?"

"Well, let there be no mistake," said the courageous patriot, and he signed in bold letters, "Charles Carroll of Carollton."

In the final chapter of his book *Profiles in Courage* the late President John F. Kennedy wrote:

> Without belittling the courage with which men have died, we should not forget those acts of courage with which men . . .have lived. The courage of life is often a less dramatic spectacle than the courage of a final moment; but it is no less a magnificent mixture of triumph and tragedy. A man does what he must . . . —in spite of personal consequences, in spite of obstacles and dangers and pressures—and that is the basis of all human morality.[4]

Courage and honesty are marks of true greatness. These make the light of a civilization burn brightly! The question is, Can we restigmatize dishonesty and magnify honesty?

Third, John the Baptist possessed purity and faith. From birth John was set apart to live a moral life. John was a good man. The prophecy concerning him was: "He . . . shall drink neither wine or strong drink; and he shall be filled with the Holy Ghost" (Luke 1:15). John knew about purity, goodness, and discipline. He lived in the wilderness and ate locusts and wild honey. His purpose was to direct men to Jesus Christ. John had a reason to live. He was the forerunner of Christ. He was the one who showed the way to the Lord Jesus, and he lived his life and carried out his mission in purity.

Will Durant, one of today's most respected philosopher-historians, said, "The greatest question of our time is not Communism versus individualism, not Europe versus America, not even the East versus the West; it is whether men can bear to live without God. Can civilization hold together if man abandons his faith in God?"

Psalm 11:3 asks the question, "If the foundations be destroyed, what can the righteous do?" In his book *Man's Search for Himself,* Dr. Rollo May quotes Friedrich Nietzsche, who wrote a parable about the death of God. It is a haunting story about a madman who ran into the village square shouting, "Where is God?" The people around him did not believe in God; they laughed and said that perhaps God had gone on a voyage or emigrated. The madman then shouted, "Where is God? I shall tell you! We have killed Him—you and I—yet how have we done this? . . . Who gave us the sponge to wipe away the whole horizon? What did we do when we unchained this earth from its sun? . . . Whither shall we move now? Away from all suns? Do we not fall incessantly? Backward, sideward, forward, in all directions? Is there yet any up and down?"[5]

Nietzsche was not calling for a return to conventional belief in God, but his story serves to point to what happens when a nation loses its center of values. "If the foundations be destroyed, what can the righteous do?"

George Bernard Shaw, a critic of the Christian faith, wrote, "This I know—men without religion are moral cowards. The cause of Europe's miseries was its lack of religion."

Voltaire, the French infidel, is reported to have said in connection with achieving a regulated society, "If there were no God, it would be necessary to invent Him."

All these men, although we would reject their overall philosophies, were right in one regard. According to the Bible, nations fall because they turn from God and from His Word. They attempt to build an adequate way of life by their own efforts and without regard to God. The cycle of rise and collapse that we see in history is the inevitable result.

But there is an alternative; there is hope. Our country does not need to fall. If the cause of collapse is turning *from* God, the remedy lies in turning *to* God. Can we do this? Yes. First we can cry out to God for help in returning to Him. Three times in Psalm 80 the writer, in a seeming agony of urgency, seeks this kind of favor. "Turn us, O God," he pleads, "and cause thy face to shine; and we shall be saved." We need God's help and mercy even to seek Him. We who belong to God must ask Him to send revival to His people. Lukewarm, half-hearted, apathetic Christians are the greatest obstacle to renewal in our country.

As individuals we can commit ourselves anew to honesty and integrity. We can seek a spirit of humility and genuine readiness to serve. We can speak out for higher standards of morality, contending for the truth in every circumstance and situation. But especially we can ask God to help us proclaim Jesus Christ as God's eternal Lamb, who alone can meet the need of cleansing from sin and the new birth.

We must reach individauls with the message of the gospel. That is God's way, His program for our age. What, after all, are dying civilizations but the sum total of dying individual lives? Never underestimate what God can do through you as an individual. But you must begin by letting Him make you a Christlike person, a man or woman with a quality of holy life that cannot go unnoticed.

That was the characteristic Woodrow Wilson noted in the great evangelist D. L. Moody. Speaking at Princeton University before he became President of the United States, Mr. Wilson said of Moody:

> I was in a very plebian place. I was in a barber's shop, sitting in a chair, when I became aware that a personality had entered the room. A man had come quietly in upon the same errand as myself and sat in the next chair to me. Every word he uttered, though it was not in the least didactic, showed a personal and vital interest in the man who was serving him; and before I got through with what was being done to me, I was aware that I had attended an evangelistic service, because Mr. Moody was in the next chair. I purposely lingered in the room after he left and noted the singular effect his visit had upon the barbers in that shop. They talked in undertones. They did not know his name, but they knew that something had elevated their thought. And I felt that I left that place as I should have left a place of worship.[6]

God can do great things through consecrated individuals, through yielded lives. Ask Jesus Christ to light the light that makes our nation great. Ask Him to begin with you right now.

Notes

1. John W. Gardner, *No Easy Victories* (New York: Harper & Row, 1970), p. 13.
2. Ibid., p. 16.
3. William Lederer and Eugene Burdick, *The Ugly American* (New York: Fawcett, 1971), p. 144.
4. John F. Kennedy, *Profiles in Courage* (New York: Harper & Row, 1964), p. 216.
5. Rollo May, *Man's Search for Himself* (New York: Dell, 1973), p. 54.
6. As quoted in John McDowell, *Dwight L. Moody* (New York: Revell, 1915), pp. 38-39.

14

Why Christians Need the Poor

"When you have enemies like hunger, poverty, and disease," declares a young man from Bangladesh, "you have no choice but to fight. You fight to be born and fight to stay alive!" The battle of poverty goes on and on. Most of us, the world would say, are among the winners. But what should Christians do about the poverty of others?

WHO ARE THE POOR?

Mattie Schultz is a white-haired widow, now ninety-one years old. She is the kind of person you would expect to keep a well-filled cookie jar for children who call her "grandma."

Yet, just last summer in her home city of San Antonio, Texas, she was lodged overnight in jail. The charge was shoplifting. She was accused of taking $15.04 worth of ham, sausage, and butter to keep from starving.[1]

Within a few days after newspapers and television stations had told her story, offers to help came pouring in. But the fact that such a thing could happen reminds us that in spite of all our relief and help programs, the poor are still among us.

Not many years ago, shortly before the Christmas season, a little paperback book appeared. It was filled with thumbnail sketches of the poor for whom there would be no Christmas. The poor spoke for themselves. They told how it felt to be without such things as underwear, soap, and toothpaste when the world around exchanges presents.

By virtually every standard, ours is the most affluent country in the world. We spend billions on relief and welfare. Yet millions among us know the ache of poverty. In 1964 President Lyndon Johnson, as part of his dream for what he called the "Great Society," declared unconditional war on poverty. But poverty did not disappear. In 1976, after spending hundreds of billions of dollars to fight poverty, the country was told by the Census Bureau that more than one in every ten Americans must be considered poor.[2]

Overseas the pinch of poverty is worse. *Time* magazine, not long ago, declared that nearly thirty out of every one hundred persons worldwide barely keep from starving. Millions struggle for existence on a per capita income of less than $200 a year! The World Food Council tells us that a third of the children in the world die of malnutrition and disease before they have five birthdays. Each year 100,000 children go blind because of lack of vitamin A in their early diets.[3] Shocking, isn't it?

WHY DO WE HAVE THE POOR?

Why are things like that still true today? Why is it that society, in spite of all its resources, has never solved the poverty problems? There are a number of reasons. One obviously is individual differences. Some poor people are strong, aggressive, clever—even ruthless. Some are less capable. Some encounter adversity. Health may fail, accidents may strike, opportunities may be denied. Great numbers begin this life as underprivileged people, never rising above the disadvantaged group.

More important, the Bible seems to say that God allows the poor among us to test our compassion for our fellow men. Do we really love the poor? Will we help in their need? Our response to poverty reveals our attitude.

Some have wrongly assumed that to be poor is a sign of God's disfavor. That is not true. God loves the poor and cares for them. He hears their cry. He sees and judges those who wrong them in their weakness. Speaking of the poor, the psalmist says, "The Lord is his refuge" (Psalm 14:6). God sees and cares and intervenes. God "setteth . . . the poor on high from affliction," says Psalm 107:41, "and maketh him families like a flock."

Likewise, the Word of God teaches that God will bless those who reach out to help the poor. "Blessed is he that considereth the poor," we read in Psalm 41:1. "The Lord will deliver him in time of trouble." On the other hand, we invite God's judgment if we ignore the needs of the poor. Proverbs 21:13 declares, "Whoso stoppeth his ears at the cry of the poor, he also shall cry himself, but shall not be heard."

If God loves the poor, if He is concerned about their needs, if He leaves the poor among us to prove our love and compassion, we as Christians cannot ignore the poor.

How Can We Help the Poor?

The question is not whether Christians should help the poor, but *how?* Some contend that we should find some way to redistribute wealth and thus wipe out all poverty.

I do not see that as Christ's will or as an answer to the ultimate poverty problem. To be sure, Christ taught that Christians are not to hoard riches. He taught that we should share. Nothing in Scripture, however, suggests that Christians can or should change the world's economic structure itself or eliminate poverty. On the contrary, Jesus clearly taught that poverty goes with this present evil world. "Ye have the poor with you always," He said in Mark, chapter 14.

Christ's principle of ministry to the poor is that it be done from a heart of genuine compassion. In His Sermon on the Mount in Matthew 6, Jesus taught not only that helping the poor should be done—He said, *"When* ye do alms," not "if"—but also that it should be done without fanfare. Christ regarded giving to the poor as normal.

Just what was Christ's program for the poor? It included justice, for the whole of Scripture sets that standard. But beyond that, He urged compassion and simple sharing. Such sharing demands awareness of need.

In the Old Testament economy of God, poverty was not wiped out, but the poor were given special protection. A poor worker was paid each day. If a poor man borrowed, giving his robe as security, the garment was to be returned before the owner needed it for warmth that night. Persons who sold themselves as servants were freed each seventh year. If lands were sold, they could be redeemed by relatives. If not redeemed, they automatically reverted to their former owners every fifty years in the Year of Jubilee.

Anyone willing to work was assured of food to feed his family. It could be obtained by gleaning in fields, where produce was left deliberately for that purpose. The Old Testament book of Ruth describes how Ruth and her mother-in-law, Naomi, lived on such gleanings.

In New Testament times, the Jewish poor were less protected by laws. The duty of giving alms, however, was acknowledged and encouraged. Jesus often spoke of giving to the poor. The record of the early church is filled with references to Christian compassion for the poor, especially to fellow believers. Widows without support were cared for by the church, as seen in Acts 6:1 and 1 Timothy 5:9,16. The poor were a subject of special concern at the first church council in Jerusalem. Paul mentions them in Galatians 2:10, where he writes that church leaders desired "that we should remember the poor." And then he adds, "The same which I also was forward [eager] to do."

Christians have always been God's special channel of mercy to the poor. But we should not lose sight of the fact that God blesses us as we carry out this ministry.

WHY SHOULD WE HELP THE POOR?

The poor are good for Christians in at least three ways. *First, the presence of the poor prompts us to exercise compassion.* How selfish and self-centered we become when we think just of ourselves! The presence of the poor is a constant challenge to be concerned about the needs of others.

Christians have been called out to demonstrate God's love. The needs of our world are our concern. God's love is to be shown in tangible, practical ways. John writes in 1 John 3:17, "But whoso hath this world's good . . . and [closes his heart against him], how dwelleth the love of God in him? . . . Let us not love in word . . . but in deed and in truth." John is speaking here of love for fellow Christians. But Christian love is to reach beyond the confines of church membership.

So Paul wrote the church in Thessalonica, "The Lord make you to increase and abound in love toward one another and toward all men" (1 Thessalonians 3:12). As the church ministers to the poor, inside its membership or outside, it demonstrates God's love.

Jesus taught that the will of God can be summed up in two great commandments—love God and love your neighbor. If we would do the will of God, we must have compassion on the poor.

Second, the presence of the poor gives us opportunity to prove that Christ has touched our hearts and made them new. Helping the poor, especially when it costs in time and money, is not a natural instinct. Instead, our old sin natures prompt us to look the other way. Compassion, on the other hand, is an evidence of an inner work of grace.

The apostle James speaks of faith and works. Real faith produces works. Our acts are proof of faith. The Christian who helps the poor proves beyond the shadow of a doubt that he shares the life and love of Christ.

Third, the poor give Christians opportunity to lay up heavenly treasure. "He that hath pity upon the poor lendeth to the LORD," says Proverbs 19:17. "And that which he hath given will he pay him again." To give to the poor for Jesus' sake is to invest money in heaven. Not only is such treasure safe from moth and rust, but it helps our hearts to be fixed on heaven as well. "For where your treasure is," Christ said, "there will your heart be also." It is not just a duty for the Christian to help the poor. In the wisdom of God, helping the poor is a blessing and a privilege.

There is a practical side to helping the poor. How should a church reach out? The first concern of any church is for the poor among its members. Does some fellow Christian struggle under the burden of inadequate housing? Has sickness brought financial crisis? The church can help in such a situation. Are children in need of clothing? Is someone out of work? The church should be concerned. Many churches have special funds for providing material help. Often these can be used to relieve a needy situation.

But individual Christians also have an obligation. If I see a need within my power to meet, I have no right to turn away. God will help me if I share in love and trust that God will meet my needs as I give generously to others.

We dare not turn our backs on the world's needs. The apostle James warns in James 2:15-16, "If a brother or sister be naked, and destitute of daily food, and one of you say unto them, Depart in peace, be ye warmed and filled; notwithstanding ye give them not those things needful to the body; what shall it profit?"

That is the attitude of the world, not the outlook of the Christian. The Christian is to love, to care, and to show compassion, even at the cost of sacrifice.

Could there be someone in your church who needs more or better food? Someone who needs to see the dentist or be fitted for glasses? Does some family need warmer winter outfits for their children? It may be your opportunity to minister—perhaps your chance to win a blessing.

The same principles hold for those we encounter outside the circle of church membership. If we see a need and it lies within our power to be of help, we have responsibility to help. The person involved may be a neighbor down the street. Or we may share in some united effort to help the disadvantaged in a worthy way. Neither the church as a body nor individual Christians can turn away from need, wherever it may be.

And then there is the yawning chasm of worldwide need. The church as a whole, and every member of the church, can have part in helping somewhere in our world. The need is so great that we cannot respond to every need, but we can help generously with some. Jesus told his disciples, "Freely ye have received; freely give." Our first and great obligation, of course, is to share the

Bread of Life. But we cannot withhold the bread of material aid when it lies within our power to give it.

Jesus told two parables that may help us see our obligation. The first, recorded in Luke 16, was about a rich man and a beggar. The rich man, Jesus said, lived out his life in luxury. In time he died and went to hell—not merely because he had been rich, of course, but because he had been satisfied with riches and had looked no further. The poor man had lived out his life unnoticed at the rich man's very doorstep.

The parable teaches the folly of trusting riches, but it also should remind us that the poor are all around us. Like the rich man we can shut them out, or like Christ we can help them in compassion.

The other parable is the story of the Good Samaritan. Three travelers in succession saw a man in a desperate plight. He had been robbed, beaten, and left beside the road to die. Two of the men who passed by the victim professed to be religious. But they did not want to get involved. The third, a Samaritan, took the time and trouble to help. He bound up the wounds of the injured man and brought him to a place of safety. He even arranged to pay his bills until the victim was back on his feet.

The church collectively and Christians as individuals have been called to be good neighbors. We cannot prevent the tragedies of life that leave poor people by the wayside. Nor can we help them all. But we can help some of the needy—those that are within our reach.

Let us recall the two kinds of attitudes—the rich man lived a lifetime indifferent to the beggar on his doorstep; the Samaritan in a moment of opportunity chose to make himself a blessing. God's call to us is to be like the Good Samaritan. We need to be willing to share salvation and material aid with our fellowmen.

NOTES

1. *Chicago Tribune*, 21 July 1979.
2. *Newsweek*, 9 October 1978, pp. 54,56
3. *Chicago Tribune*, 4 December 1978.

Moody Press, a ministry of the Moody Bible Institute, is designed for education, evangelization, and edification. If we may assist you in knowing more about Christ and the Christian life, please write us without obligation: Moody Press, c/o MLM, Chicago, Illinois 60610.